Betty Crocker

just the two of us

More than 130 Delicious Recipes to Enjoy Together

BICENTENNIAL
1807
WILEY
2007
BICENTENNIAL

Wiley Publishing, Inc.

For general information on our other products and services or to obtain technical support please contact our Customer Care Department within the U.S. at 800-762-2974, outside the U.S. at 317-572-3993 or fax 317-572-4002.

Wiley also publishes its books in a variety of electronic formats. Some content that appears in print may not be available in electronic books. For more information about Wiley products, visit our web site at www.wiley.com.

Library of Congress Cataloging-in-Publication Data:

Betty Crocker just the two of us : More than 130 delicious recipes to enjoy together.
        p. cm.
    Includes index.
    ISBN: 978-0-471-99793-1 (cloth)
  1. Cookery for two.   I. Crocker, Betty.
    TX652.B4972 2007
    641.5'61--dc22

                                                            2006036936

Manufactured in the United States of America

10 9 8 7 6 5 4 3 2 1

Wiley Bicentennial Logo: Richard J. Pacifico

General Mills
PUBLISHER, BOOKS AND MAGAZINES: Sheila Burke
MANAGER, COOKBOOK PUBLISHING: Lois Tlusty
SENIOR EDITOR: Cheri Olerud
FOOD EDITOR: Andi Bidwell
RECIPE DEVELOPMENT AND TESTING: Betty
    Crocker Kitchens
PHOTOGRAPHY AND FOOD STYLING: General Mills
    Photography Studios and Image Library
PHOTOGRAPHER: Val Bourassa
FOOD STYLISTS: Amy Peterson and Sue Brosious

Wiley Publishing, Inc.
PUBLISHER: Natalie Chapman
EXECUTIVE EDITOR: Anne Ficklen
EDITOR: Kristi Hart
EDITORIAL ASSISTANT: Charleen Barila
SENIOR PRODUCTION EDITOR: Alda Trabucchi
ART DIRECTOR: Tai Blanche
COVER DESIGN: Paul Dinovo
INTERIOR DESIGN AND LAYOUT: Laura Ierardi
MANUFACTURING MANAGER: Kevin Watt

The Betty Crocker Kitchens seal guarantees success in your kitchen. Every recipe has been tested in America's Most Trusted Kitchens™ to meet our high standards of reliability, easy preparation and great taste.

FIND MORE GREAT IDEAS AT

Betty Crocker.com

COVER PHOTO: Mediterranean Grilled Snapper (page 89);
PHOTO ON PAGE 4: ©istockphoto/jkey;
PHOTO ON PAGE 5: ©istockphoto/pkgraphics;
PHOTO ON PAGE 6: ©istockphoto/matejmm;
PHOTO ON PAGE 7: ©Corbis Digital Stock; PHOTO ON PAGE 8: ©istockphoto/og-vision; PHOTO ON PAGE 211: ©Digital Vision;
PHOTO ON PAGE 212: ©PhotoDisc;
PHOTO ON PAGE 213: ©GM;
PHOTO ON PAGE 215: ©istockphoto/alohashaka

Dear Friends,

Aren't you excited? You've reached the time in your life where you're cooking for just two. Forget trying to please everyone, getting the kids to eat their vegetables and serving the same foods week after week. Now, the grown-ups rule!

You're an experienced cook, but you may find cooking for two a challenge—finding recipes or downsizing your favorite recipes can take more time than you want to spend or not seem worth the effort.

Relax, we have the easy answer. All the recipes in this cookbook were developed for exactly two. Not three, not four or six, but two people. And, in true Betty Crocker style, the recipes are simple, easy, good for you—and taste terrific.

Want to bake smaller batches of cookies, muffins, bars? They're here. Searching for quick skillet meals? They're here. Enticing Cozy Casseroles, made just for two? They're here too.

You'll also be pleasantly surprised by the easy vegetables, fresh-tasting salads and yummy soups that turn "two" into terrific! Of course delicious desserts, created for two are also included—so you have just the perfect amount.

Cooking for two can be an opportunity to make exciting lifestyle—and recipe—changes. Look for the many tips and beneficial information throughout the book to lend you a hand.

Here's to the two of you!

Betty Crocker

Contents

Cooking for Two

Congratulations!

You're back to cooking for two. No more worries about pleasing picky eaters! As an experienced cook who has juggled the demands of cooking for a family for years, you may find that smaller-size cooking can be a challenge. Selecting recipes that serve only two are often not easy to find. Maybe you're wondering how to downsize your favorite recipes. To add to that, kitchen equipment and ingredients are often not geared for small-size recipes or households.

Now's the time to make a new discovery—cooking for two is an opportunity to find and try new recipes, new ingredients, new products and new equipment that will make it easier to cook just the right amount for two portions.

Shopping and cooking for two can be really fun. Just think—you can:

- buy what the two of you really like.
- splurge on more expensive items because the quantity is smaller.
- be as creative as you have time for and experiment more.

There are new foods, new ideas, new recipes and new flavors just waiting for you.

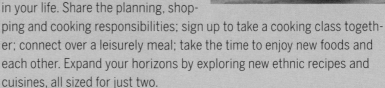

Tea for Two

Let this be the time to reconnect with your spouse or that special someone in your life. Share the planning, shopping and cooking responsibilities; sign up to take a cooking class together; connect over a leisurely meal; take the time to enjoy new foods and each other. Expand your horizons by exploring new ethnic recipes and cuisines, all sized for just two.

Where Do I Start?

Want to make a few adjustments to your pantry, shopping, planning and cooking? Let these tips help you make the most of your time:

1. Equip Your Kitchen

Small-size equipment is becoming more available, and you may find it a lifesaver. As you downsize your kitchen, look for new appliances and pans to freshen up your favorite room in the house. You'll find that the colors and patterns are prettier and brighter than ever before. Check out this list to help you cook and bake small amounts more efficiently:

- 6-cup muffin pans
- Smaller cookie sheets
- 8-inch square baking pans
- 8-inch nonstick fluted tube (bundt cake) pans
- 4-inch tube pans for baking angel food cakes
- Set of small custard cups (6-ounce size) or 4- to 6-ounce ramekins for individual desserts
- 1-quart casseroles
- 2-cup (16-ounce) and 3-cup (24-ounce) baking dishes
- Small coffeemaker that brews 2 or 4 cups of coffee
- Toaster oven

- Contact grill
- Small food chopper
- Small slow cookers (1 1/2- to 2-quart size)
- Mini loaf pans for meat loaves, quick breads and bars
- Sturdy food-storage containers (1- to 3-cup size) for leftovers

2. Explore the Store

There are many cooking-for-two choices that will fit your downsized kitchen. Add these to your grocery list to bring convenience to your cooking:

Meat items, like two pork chops, chicken breasts or 1/2 pound ground beef are usually available. If you don't find them, ask the butcher.

Individually frozen servings of fruits, vegetables, chicken breasts or tenders, fish fillets and shrimp that allow you to use only the amount you need.

Frozen biscuits and rolls, either in two-serve packages or a bag that allows you to use just a few at a time.

Frozen meals and prepackaged single-serving foods like instant oatmeal, canned soups, seasoned rice and pasta.

Smaller quantity and size of already-cut fruit in the fruit section.

Bulk bins that let you select only the amount you need of nuts, trail mix, grains, dried pasta, rice, lentils, granola.

Eggs by the half-dozen (or frozen egg substitute product).

Smaller cans of soups, sauces, fruits, beans and vegetables.

Smaller portions of deli items, like mashed potatoes, specialty cheeses, cooked chicken breasts, pasta and potato salads, dinners and desserts.

Small amounts from the salad bar, like fresh veggies, salad greens, sliced cucumbers, shredded carrots, pea pods. Use these ingredients not only in salads but also as sides and in soups and stir-fries.

Olive bars for two (or ten, if you're having a party) at some of the larger supermarkets.

3. Cook and Store Wisely

Plan for Leftovers

As long as you're cooking, save time by planning meals that use the extra food in other dishes.

Cook rice or pasta as a side dish for one meal, then use the leftover rice or pasta in a casserole or soup.

Bake three or four chicken breasts, use two for a meal and the extra for sandwiches, soup or a stir-fry.

Make a regular-size meat loaf mixture, and divide it in half. Use half for meat loaf, and cook the other half as meatballs to partner with pasta and sauce another night.

Make a double batch of chili. Eat it the first night as chili; serve the remaining batch another night over pasta as Cincinnati chili.

Use Your Freezer

Most foods freeze well, including soups, casseroles, breads, meats, vegetables, whole grains, nuts and seeds. Baked goods are especially suitable for freezing. To freeze, store food in moisture-proof containers such as foil, freezer bags, freezer wrap and plastic freezer containers, removing as much air as possible.

"Batch Cook" Meals in Advance

If your usual recipe makes four or six servings, take advantage of the extra amount and freeze in single or double portions.

Prepare One-Dish Meals

Choose a dish that includes foods from several food groups: meat, whole grains, legumes and vegetables, like beef-barley stew; salmon, rice and veggie packets; turkey and bean casserole.

Cook with a Friend

Share shopping and cooking with a friend who also cooks for two. Or exchange cooked dishes with a friend for a little variety. Split foods that come packaged for four. Freeze meals to use later.

4. Know What to Keep on Hand

Having the right ingredients in your new-for-two kitchen can make cooking quicker, easier and more fun. The key is to buy foods in smaller sizes. If you're looking for a smaller size and can't find it, buy the smallest size you can find and separate it into serving-size portions.

Stock your cupboard, refrigerator and freezer with the favorites you use frequently, and tuck away a few items for impromptu entertaining (like fancy store-bought cookies, sorbet, premium frozen yogurt or ice cream, frozen shrimp, olives, Alfredo sauce, pesto, focaccia, pizza).

Essentials to keep on hand:

- Quick-cooking grains
- Dried pasta and flavored rice mixes
- Individual packets of oatmeal
- Tuna in water (3-ounce can or pouch)
- Vegetables (8-ounce cans)
- Small sizes of canned fruits or individual containers of fruit or applesauce
- Ready-to-serve soups in cans or individual containers
- Dried herbs and spices from the bulk section (keep in a dark place, refrigerate or freeze)

- Tubes of tomato paste, tomato puree, green pesto
- Individual packets of dry salad dressing mixes
- Seasoning mixes (keep a variety on hand, like Cajun, Creole, Greek and jerk); freeze for longer storage
- Individual packages of puddings and applesauce
- Snack cakes, muffin mixes, dessert mixes in small pouches
- Small packages of sugar and flour (2-pound size) if you don't bake a lot
- Single-serve bags and small-size cans of chips and snacks
- Tea and coffee in single-serving sizes

Top Cooking and Baking **Q** & **A**

Here are the answers to frequently asked cooking and baking questions for two:

Q. I bought Splenda® Sugar Blend for Baking. How do I bake with it?

A. Splenda Sugar Blend for Baking is a blend of brown sugar and sucralose, an artificial sweetener. It is designed to use in baked goods, where sugar also has a major role in the baked goods' characteristics, like volume, browning, amount of rise, texture and moistness (as in cookies, bars, brownies and breads). When using it, your baked goods may bake more quickly, or there may be other changes. Splenda No Calorie Sweetener (Granular) offers more calorie savings and works best in foods that use sugar only for sweetness, like pies, sauces, marinades and glazes. Read the package directions on each of those products before using them and follow what the manufacturer recommends in your favorite recipes. For more information, visit the Splenda web site at www.splenda.com or call 1-800-7-Splenda.

Q. Can I use egg product substitutes in place of eggs? How do I use them?

A. The recipes in this cookbook were tested with large eggs. Also available are reduced-cholesterol eggs, sold in the shell. Egg product substitute, which comes in frozen or refrigerated cartons, has egg whites as the main ingredient. You can use egg whites or egg product substitutes instead of whole eggs to reduce the cholesterol in your favorite recipes and the recipes in this cookbook. For best results, use 1/4 cup egg product substitute for 1 egg, or follow package directions. Two egg whites are equal to one whole egg.

Q. I've been hearing a lot about canola oil. Why is it so good? Is olive oil still a good oil to use?

A. Canola oil is the most popular cooking oil in America. Because it's high in monounsaturated fats (the "good" fats that are believed to help lower cholesterol) and low in saturated fats (the "bad" fats that are thought to raise cholesterol). Canola oil also contains omega-3 fatty acids, a polyunsaturated fat found in fatty fish like salmon and sardines and in vegetable oils like canola, soybean and flaxseed. Omega-3 fatty acids are thought to have heart-health benefits.

Canola oil works well for baking and stir-frying. Olive oil is also a very good oil because of its high monounsaturated-fat content and low saturated-fat content, and it works well in most recipes. Olive oil is often used in savory recipes rather than sweet ones because of its distinct flavor. Olive oil does not contain omega-3 fatty acids.

Q. I have a lot of favorite recipes that serve more than two. How do I cut those recipes down?

A. First, consider whether cutting down the quantity is what you want to do. If you are used to making a recipe that serves four, for instance, you could make the same quantity and freeze the remaining servings, either in individual or for-two quantities. When you do want to cut the quantity of a larger recipe, use this handy chart to help you decide how to decrease the ingredients.

Decreasing Ingredients

Original Amount	Half the Recipe	One-third the Recipe
1/4 teaspoon	1/8 teaspoon	Dash
1/2 teaspoon	1/4 teaspoon	1/8 teaspoon
1 teaspoon	1/2 teaspoon	1/4 teaspoon
1 tablespoon	1 1/2 teaspoons	1 teaspoon
1/4 cup	2 tablespoons	1 tablespoon plus 1 teaspoon
1/3 cup	2 tablespoons plus 2 teaspoons	1 tablespoon plus 1 1/4 teaspoons
1/2 cup	1/4 cup	2 tablespoons plus 2 teaspoons
2/3 cup	1/3 cup	3 tablespoons plus 1 1/2 teaspoons
3/4 cup	6 tablespoons	1/4 cup
1 cup	1/2 cup	1/3 cup

When baking:
- You'll need a smaller-size pan for bars. For the recipes in this cookbook, loaf pans (9 × 5-inch or 8 × 4-inch) have worked well.
- Baked goods may bake in less time, so check your bars and breads 5 to 10 minutes sooner than you would for a regular-size recipe.
- When cutting 1 egg in half, you have several choices: use egg product substitute (2 tablespoons per 1/2 egg); beat 1 egg, measure the beaten egg in a measuring cup and use half the amount; or with a bit different result, you can use 1 egg white.
- When baking desserts, consider using individual pans, like ramekins or custard cups.

When cooking:
- Consider using a smaller skillet, like 8-inch or 6-inch, or a smaller-size casserole dish, like 1-quart, depending on the quantity of food.
- Smaller quantities may cook in less time, so check your stir-fries and other skillet dishes about 5 minutes sooner than if you were cooking a larger quantity.

Bagel Tuna Melt (page 18)

Mini Meals and On-the-Go Snacks

Hawaiian Quesadillas

Prep Time: 20 minutes | **Start to Finish:** 20 minutes | 2 servings

4 flour tortillas (7 inch)

2 teaspoons reduced-fat mayonnaise or salad dressing

3 oz thinly sliced cooked ham, cut into strips

1/2 cup well-drained crushed pineapple (from 8-oz can)

1/2 cup chopped green bell pepper

1/4 cup finely shredded mozzarella cheese (1 oz)

1 In 12-inch nonstick skillet, place tortilla. Spread with 1 teaspoon of the mayonnaise. Top with half of the ham, pineapple, bell pepper and cheese. Top with second tortilla.

2 Cook over medium heat 2 to 4 minutes, turning once, until lightly browned. Remove from skillet.

3 Repeat to make second quesadilla.

tip for *two*

Give your quesadillas an extra Hawaiian touch by adding 1 teaspoon flaked coconut to the filling for each quesadilla. Use the leftover pineapple to top your bagel and cream cheese in the morning.

1 Serving: Calories 370 (Calories from Fat 100); Total Fat 12g (Saturated Fat 4g; Trans Fat 1g); Cholesterol 30mg; Sodium 930mg; Total Carbohydrate 47g (Dietary Fiber 3g; Sugars 10g); Protein 19g   **% Daily Value:** Vitamin A 4%; Vitamin C 30%; Calcium 20%; Iron 15%   **Exchanges:** 2 Starch, 1 Other Carbohydrate, 2 Lean Meat, 1 Fat
Carbohydrate Choices: 3

Quesadilla Bites

Prep Time: 15 minutes | **Start to Finish:** 15 minutes | 2 servings (3 quesadilla wedges and 2 tablespoons sauce each)

2 flour tortillas (6 inch)

12 thin slices turkey pepperoni (3/4 oz)

1 medium plum (Roma) tomato, thinly sliced

1/4 cup shredded pizza cheese blend (1 oz)

1/2 teaspoon canola oil

1/4 cup pizza sauce (from 8-oz can), warmed

1 Top 1 tortilla with pepperoni, tomato and cheese. Top with remaining tortilla.

2 In 10-inch nonstick skillet, heat oil over medium heat; rotate skillet so oil coats bottom of skillet. Cook quesadilla in oil 4 to 6 minutes, turning once, until lightly browned. Remove from skillet; place on cutting board.

3 Cut quesadilla into 6 wedges. Serve with warmed pizza sauce.

tip for *two*

Customize these bite-size appetizers with your favorite pizza toppings.

1 Serving: Calories 180 (Calories from Fat 70); Total Fat 8g (Saturated Fat 3.5g; Trans Fat 0g); Cholesterol 20mg; Sodium 570mg; Total Carbohydrate 17g (Dietary Fiber 1g; Sugars 3g); Protein 9g **% Daily Value:** Vitamin A 8%; Vitamin C 4%; Calcium 15%; Iron 10% **Exchanges:** 1 Starch, 1 High-Fat Meat **Carbohydrate Choices:** 1

Easy Pizzettes

Prep Time: 5 minutes | Start to Finish: 15 minutes | 2 servings

2 tablespoons pizza sauce

1 English muffin, split, toasted

1/4 cup shredded reduced-fat provolone cheese (1 oz)

Assorted toppings (1 tablespoon each sliced mushrooms, sliced ripe olives, chopped bell pepper and chopped red onion)

1 Heat oven to 425°F. Spread 1 tablespoon pizza sauce over each English muffin half. Sprinkle each with 1 tablespoon of the cheese. Arrange toppings on pizzas. Sprinkle with remaining cheese.

2 Place on ungreased cookie sheet. Bake 5 to 10 minutes or until cheese is melted.

tip for *two*

To increase the amount of whole grains you eat, try whole wheat English muffins in this easy recipe. Mozzarella cheese can be used in place of the provolone cheese.

1 Serving: Calories 120 (Calories from Fat 30); Total Fat 3g (Saturated Fat 1.5g; Trans Fat 0g); Cholesterol 0mg; Sodium 290mg; Total Carbohydrate 16g (Dietary Fiber 1g; Sugars 5g); Protein 7g   **% Daily Value:** Vitamin A 2%; Vitamin C 4%; Calcium 15%; Iron 6%   **Exchanges:** 1 Other Carbohydrate, 1 Lean Meat   **Carbohydrate Choices:** 1

Bagel Tuna Melt

Prep Time: 10 minutes | **Start to Finish:** 10 minutes | 2 servings

1 whole-grain or whole wheat bagel, cut in half

1 can (6 oz) tuna in water, drained

2 tablespoons reduced-fat mayonnaise or salad dressing

1 teaspoon yellow mustard

1 medium green onion, sliced (1 tablespoon)

1/4 medium apple, thinly sliced

2 slices reduced-fat process sharp Cheddar cheese

1 Set oven control to broil. On cookie sheet, place bagel halves, cut sides up. Broil with tops 4 to 5 inches from heat 1 to 2 minutes or until desired brownness.

2 In small bowl, mix tuna, mayonnaise, mustard and onion. Divide tuna mixture between bagel halves. Top with apple and cheese slices.

3 Broil 1 to 2 minutes longer or until cheese is melted and tuna is warm.

See photo on page 12

tip for *two*

Use pear slices instead of the apple slices in this easy, tasty sandwich. For a quick lunch, add baked potato chips, baby-cut carrots and a glass of fat-free (skim) milk.

1 Serving: Calories 280 (Calories from Fat 80); Total Fat 9g (Saturated Fat 3g; Trans Fat 0g); Cholesterol 40mg; Sodium 820mg; Total Carbohydrate 24g (Dietary Fiber 2g; Sugars 7g); Protein 27g   **% Daily Value:** Vitamin A 6%; Vitamin C 0%; Calcium 15%; Iron 15%   **Exchanges:** 1/2 Starch, 1 Other Carbohydrate, 3 1/2 Very Lean Meat, 1 1/2 Fat **Carbohydrate Choices:** 1 1/2

Tuna in Pitas

Prep Time: 5 minutes | **Start to Finish:** 5 minutes | 2 servings

1 tablespoon finely chopped onion

2 tablespoons finely chopped celery

2 tablespoons reduced-fat mayonnaise or salad dressing

1/2 teaspoon curry powder

1 can (3 oz) light tuna in water, drained

2 lettuce leaves

1 whole wheat pita bread, cut in half to form pockets

1/2 medium orange, cut into 1/2-inch pieces

1 In small bowl, mix onion, celery, mayonnaise and curry powder. Stir in tuna.

2 Place lettuce leaf in each pita bread half; fill with tuna mixture. Top with orange pieces.

tip for *two*

Make it Chicken Salad in Pitas by using 1/2 cup cut-up cooked chicken instead of the tuna. Add a serving of plain fat-free yogurt, a few slices of cucumber and a glass of sparkling water for a refreshing lunch.

1 Serving: Calories 230 (Calories from Fat 110); Total Fat 12g (Saturated Fat 2g; Trans Fat 0g); Cholesterol 15mg; Sodium 320mg; Total Carbohydrate 18g (Dietary Fiber 3g; Sugars 5g); Protein 12g **% Daily Value:** Vitamin A 4%; Vitamin C 30%; Calcium 4%; Iron 8% **Exchanges:** 1/2 Starch, 1/2 Other Carbohydrate, 1 1/2 Very Lean Meat, 2 Fat Carbohydrate Choices: 1

Shrimp Toasts

Prep Time: 10 minutes | **Start to Finish:** 15 minutes | 2 servings (2 toasts each)

1 tablespoon olive oil

1 teaspoon grated lemon peel

1 teaspoon lemon juice

1 teaspoon honey

4 uncooked deveined peeled large (21 to 26 count) shrimp, thawed if frozen, tail shells removed

2 teaspoons butter, softened (do not use margarine)

1 teaspoon orange marmalade

4 slices baguette French bread (1/4 inch thick)

Cilantro sprigs

1 In small bowl, mix oil, lemon peel, lemon juice and honey. Add shrimp; toss to coat.

2 Set oven control to broil. In small bowl, stir butter and marmalade until well mixed. Spread butter mixture over bread slices.

3 Remove shrimp from marinade; discard marinade. On rack in broiler pan, place shrimp and bread, buttered sides up, in single layer. Broil with tops 4 to 6 inches from heat 4 to 6 minutes or until shrimp are cooked through and bread is lightly toasted.

4 Place 1 shrimp on each bread slice. Garnish with cilantro.

tip for *two*

These little shrimp toasts are the perfect tide-me-over. Vary the flavor by using lime juice and lime peel instead of lemon, and apricot preserves instead of the orange marmalade.

1 Serving: Calories 250 (Calories from Fat 70); Total Fat 8g (Saturated Fat 3g; Trans Fat 0.5g); Cholesterol 35mg; Sodium 430mg; Total Carbohydrate 35g (Dietary Fiber 2g; Sugars 3g); Protein 8g   **% Daily Value:** Vitamin A 8%; Vitamin C 0%; Calcium 6%; Iron 15%   **Exchanges:** 1 Starch, 1 1/2 Other Carbohydrate, 1/2 Very Lean Meat, 1 1/2 Fat Carbohydrate Choices: 2

Smoked Salmon and Bagels

Prep Time: 20 minutes | **Start to Finish:** 20 minutes | 2 servings

4 thin stalks asparagus (about 2 oz)

1 1/2 oz reduced-fat cream cheese (Neufchâtel), softened (about 2 rounded tablespoons)

1/2 teaspoon dried dill weed

1 teaspoon grated lemon peel

1 teaspoon lemon juice

1 bagel, cut in half horizontally

1 1/2 oz salmon lox (from 3-oz package)

Lemon wedges, if desired

1 Break off tough ends of asparagus as far down as stalks snap easily. Cut asparagus in half crosswise into about 3-inch pieces. In 3-quart saucepan or skillet, place steamer basket in 1/2 inch water. Place asparagus in basket. Heat to boiling; reduce heat. Cover; steam about 5 minutes or until crisp-tender. Immediately plunge asparagus into ice water until cold. Drain on paper towels.

2 In small bowl, mix cream cheese, dill weed, lemon peel and lemon juice until well blended. Spread on cut sides of bagel halves.

3 Arrange asparagus pieces on cream cheese mixture; top with salmon. Serve with lemon wedges.

tip for *two*

You can buy vegetables and fruits individually or in bulk so you get just the quantity you need. Two ounces of green beans can be substituted for the asparagus.

1 Serving: Calories 180 (Calories from Fat 60); Total Fat 7g (Saturated Fat 3.5g; Trans Fat 0g); Cholesterol 20mg; Sodium 440mg; Total Carbohydrate 21g (Dietary Fiber 1g; Sugars 3g); Protein 11g   **% Daily Value:** Vitamin A 10%; Vitamin C 8%; Calcium 6%; Iron 10%   **Exchanges:** 1 1/2 Starch, 1 Very Lean Meat, 1 Fat   **Carbohydrate Choices:** 1 1/2

Gorp-to-Go

Pour 2 cups any ready-to-eat cereal, 2 cups popped popcorn, 2 cups pretzels, 1/4 cup dried cranberries and 1/4 cup soy nuts into resealable food-storage plastic bag; shake until mixed.

Italian Popcorn Mix

Drizzle 3 cups popped popcorn, 1 cup pretzels and 1 cup cheese crackers with a bit of melted butter; sprinkle with garlic and onion powders and dried basil and oregano leaves or Italian seasoning.

Savory Pecans

Pour 1 tablespoon melted butter over 2 cups pecans in shallow pan; sprinkle with 1 tablespoon soy sauce and 1/4 teaspoon ground red pepper (cayenne). Bake at 350°F for 6 to 10 minutes, stirring occasionally, until nuts are toasted.

Easy Cheesy Spread

Mix whipped cream cheese, shredded Cheddar or mozzarella cheese, a bit of yellow mustard and a little Worcestershire sauce. Spread on rye or wheat bread or whole-grain crackers.

Chile and Olive Spread

Stir 1 tablespoon ranch dressing mix into softened 8-ounce package cream cheese. Add 1 small can each chopped ripe olives, chopped green chiles, drained. Stir in chopped red bell peppers or sliced celery. Spread on whole-grain rolls or crackers.

5 easy On-the-Go Snacks

Try one of these great snacks the next time you hop in the car or need an on-the-go pick-me-up.

Cinnamon-Raisin Snack Mix

Prep Time: 10 minutes | **Start to Finish:** 10 minutes | 6 servings (1/2 cup each)

2 tablespoons sugar

1/2 teaspoon ground cinnamon

2 tablespoons butter or margarine

1 cup Corn Chex® cereal

1 cup Rice Chex® cereal

1 cup Wheat Chex® cereal

1/4 cup raisins, dried cranberries or dried cherries

1 In small bowl, mix sugar and cinnamon; set aside.

2 In medium microwavable bowl, microwave butter uncovered on High about 40 seconds or until melted. Stir in cereals until evenly coated. Microwave uncovered 2 minutes, stirring after 1 minute.

3 Sprinkle half of the sugar mixture evenly over cereals; stir. Sprinkle with remaining sugar mixture; stir. Microwave uncovered 1 minute. Stir in raisins. Spread on paper towels to cool.

tip for *two*

This easy snack keeps well when stored in a zip-type bag at room temperature for a few days. If you'd like to make more at a time to keep on hand, double the ingredients.

1 Serving: Calories 140 (Calories from Fat 40); Total Fat 4g (Saturated Fat 2.5g; Trans Fat 0g); Cholesterol 10mg; Sodium 180mg; Total Carbohydrate 23g (Dietary Fiber 1g; Sugars 9g); Protein 2g **% Daily Value:** Vitamin A 8%; Vitamin C 2%; Calcium 6%; Iron 30% **Exchanges:** 1/2 Starch, 1 Other Carbohydrate, 1 Fat **Carbohydrate Choices:** 1 1/2

Sweet and Crunchy Snack Mix

Prep Time: 5 minutes | Start to Finish: 5 minutes | 6 servings (1/2 cup each)

1 1/2 cups small pretzel twists

1 cup Frosted Cheerios® cereal

1/2 cup dried banana chips

1/4 cup honey-roasted peanuts

1/4 cup candy-coated chocolate candies

In medium container, mix all ingredients.

tip for *two*

Because cereal is fortified, it's high in iron and other vitamins and minerals. Divide this snack mix into small reseal-able food-storage plastic bags for a quick take-along treat.

1 Serving: Calories 180 (Calories from Fat 50); Total Fat 6g (Saturated Fat 2g; Trans Fat 0g); Cholesterol 0mg; Sodium 240mg; Total Carbohydrate 28g (Dietary Fiber 2g; Sugars 13g); Protein 4g   **% Daily Value:** Vitamin A 2%; Vitamin C 4%; Calcium 4%; Iron 10%   **Exchanges:** 1 Starch, 1 Other Carbohydrate, 1 Fat   **Carbohydrate Choices:** 2

Peanut Butter Snack Bars

Prep Time: 15 minutes | **Start to Finish:** 1 hour 15 minutes | 6 bars

1/4 cup packed brown sugar

3 tablespoons light corn syrup or honey

2 tablespoons peanut butter

1/4 teaspoon ground cinnamon

2 cups Total® Raisin Bran cereal

1/4 cup chopped peanuts or sliced almonds

1 Grease 9 × 5-inch loaf pan with butter. In 2-quart saucepan, heat brown sugar and corn syrup just to boiling over medium heat, stirring frequently. Remove from heat.

2 Stir in peanut butter and cinnamon until smooth. Stir in cereal and peanuts until evenly coated. Press mixture firmly in pan. Let stand about 1 hour or until set. Cut into 6 bars. Store loosely covered at room temperature.

tip for *two*

This whole-grain bar is a healthy, on-the-go way to begin or end your day or to have a snack any time in between. Whole grains supply fiber and B vitamins.

1 Bar: Calories 210 (Calories from Fat 60); Total Fat 6g (Saturated Fat 1g; Trans Fat 0g); Cholesterol 0mg; Sodium 140mg; Total Carbohydrate 33g (Dietary Fiber 3g; Sugars 20g); Protein 4g   **% Daily Value:** Vitamin A 4%; Vitamin C 0%; Calcium 35%; Iron 35%   **Exchanges:** 1/2 Starch, 1 1/2 Other Carbohydrate, 1/2 High-Fat Meat, 1/2 Fat   **Carbohydrate Choices:** 2

Chocolate-Cherry Soy Smoothie

Prep Time: 5 minutes | **Start to Finish:** 2 hours 5 minutes | 2 servings (1 cup each)

1 ripe small banana, peeled, cut into 2-inch chunks

1 1/4 cups chocolate-flavored soymilk or chocolate-flavored fat-free (skim) milk

3/4 cup frozen pitted cherries

1/4 teaspoon almond extract

1 Freeze banana chunks 2 hours.

2 In blender, place frozen banana chunks and remaining ingredients. Cover; blend on high speed about 30 seconds or until smooth. Serve immediately.

tip for *two*

Be ready to make this easy, tasty smoothie by freezing ripe bananas earlier. Frozen strawberries or raspberries work in place of the cherries.

1 Serving: Calories 250 (Calories from Fat 30); Total Fat 3g (Saturated Fat 0.5g; Trans Fat 0g); Cholesterol 0mg; Sodium 75mg; Total Carbohydrate 47g (Dietary Fiber 5g; Sugars 31g); Protein 7g   **% Daily Value:** Vitamin A 8%; Vitamin C 20%; Calcium 25%; Iron 15%   **Exchanges:** 2 Starch, 1 Other Carbohydrate, 1/2 Fat   **Carbohydrate Choices:** 3

Peachy Chai Smoothies

Prep Time: 10 minutes | **Start to Finish:** 10 minutes | 2 servings (1 1/3 cups each)

3/4 cup frozen sliced peaches (from 16-oz bag), partially thawed

2 containers (6 oz each) vanilla thick & creamy low-fat yogurt

3 tablespoons chai tea latte mix (from 10-oz package)

1/2 cup fat-free (skim) milk

Ground nutmeg, if desired

1 In blender or food processor, place all ingredients except nutmeg.

2 Cover; blend on high speed about 1 minute or until smooth and creamy. Sprinkle servings with dash of nutmeg.

tip for *two*

An Indian specialty, chai is simply a blend of tea, milk and mild spices.

1 Serving: Calories 320 (Calories from Fat 30); Total Fat 3.5g (Saturated Fat 1.5g; Trans Fat 0g); Cholesterol 10mg; Sodium 230mg; Total Carbohydrate 59g (Dietary Fiber 2g; Sugars 57g); Protein 13g   **% Daily Value:** Vitamin A 25%; Vitamin C 150%; Calcium 40%; Iron 2%   **Exchanges:** 1/2 Fruit, 2 1/2 Other Carbohydrate, 1 Low-Fat Milk **Carbohydrate Choices:** 4

Grilled Stuffed Tuna Melts (page 52)

Speedy Soups and Sandwiches

Easy Cheesy Vegetable Chowder

Prep Time: 15 minutes | **Start to Finish:** 30 minutes | 2 servings (2 cups each)

2/3 cup water

1/3 cup uncooked regular long-grain white rice

2 cups fat-free (skim) milk

1/4 teaspoon chili powder

2 oz reduced-fat prepared cheese product (from 16-oz loaf), cubed

2 cups (from 1-lb bag) frozen cauliflower, carrots and snow pea pods (or other combination), thawed, drained

1 In 2-quart saucepan, heat water to boiling; stir in rice. Reduce heat to low. Cover; cook 15 minutes.

2 Stir in remaining ingredients. Heat to boiling. Cook about 5 minutes, stirring occasionally, until vegetables are tender.

tip for *two*

If you'd like to eat more whole grains, you can use brown rice in place of the white rice and just cook it longer, following package directions.

1 Serving: Calories 300 (Calories from Fat 35); Total Fat 3.5g (Saturated Fat 2.5g; Trans Fat 0g); Cholesterol 15mg; Sodium 580mg; Total Carbohydrate 48g (Dietary Fiber 4g; Sugars 17g); Protein 19g **% Daily Value:** Vitamin A 70%; Vitamin C 30%; Calcium 50%; Iron 10% **Exchanges:** 1 1/2 Starch, 1 Other Carbohydrate, 1 Skim Milk, 1 Very Lean Meat **Carbohydrate Choices:** 3

Italian Beef and Bean Soup

Prep Time: 15 minutes | **Start to Finish:** 35 minutes | 2 servings (about 1 2/3 cups each)

1 teaspoon all-purpose flour

1/8 teaspoon salt

1/8 teaspoon pepper

1/4 lb boneless beef round steak, cut into 1/2-inch cubes

2 teaspoons olive oil

1 can (15 oz) cannellini beans, drained, rinsed

1 can (14.5 oz) diced tomatoes with basil, garlic and oregano, undrained

1 cup water

Grated Parmesan cheese, if desired

1 In 1-quart resealable plastic food-storage bag, place flour, salt and pepper. Seal bag; shake until blended. Add beef. Seal bag; shake until beef is evenly coated with flour mixture.

2 In 2-quart heavy saucepan, heat oil over medium-high heat. Cook beef in oil 4 to 5 minutes, stirring occasionally, until brown on all sides.

3 Stir in remaining ingredients except cheese. Heat to boiling; reduce heat. Simmer uncovered 15 to 20 minutes or until flavors are well blended. Serve with cheese.

tip for *two*

If a whole can of beans is too much, use half a can and refrigerate the remainder to use in a salad or soup another time. Add Italian breadsticks and a bagged salad for a quick and easy meal.

1 Serving: Calories 420 (Calories from Fat 60); Total Fat 7g (Saturated Fat 1.5g; Trans Fat 0g); Cholesterol 30mg; Sodium 440mg; Total Carbohydrate 55g (Dietary Fiber 14g; Sugars 6g); Protein 33g   **% Daily Value:** Vitamin A 4%; Vitamin C 15%; Calcium 25%; Iron 60%   **Exchanges:** 2 1/2 Starch, 1/2 Other Carbohydrate, 2 Vegetable, 3 Very Lean Meat, 1 Fat   **Carbohydrate Choices:** 3 1/2

Lentil-Tofu Soup

Prep Time: 15 minutes | Start to Finish: 1 hour | 2 servings (about 1 1/2 cups each)

1 tablespoon canola oil

1 small onion, chopped (1/4 cup)

1 teaspoon curry powder

1/2 teaspoon ground cumin

1 clove garlic, finely chopped

1/3 cup dried lentils, sorted, rinsed

2 cups reduced-sodium vegetable broth (from 32-oz carton)

4 oz firm tofu (from 12-oz package), cut into 1/2-inch cubes

3/4 cup coarsely chopped broccoli

2 tablespoons chopped fresh parsley

1 In 1 1/2-quart saucepan, heat oil over medium heat. Cook onion, curry powder, cumin and garlic in oil 2 minutes, stirring occasionally. Stir in lentils and broth. Heat to boiling; reduce heat. Cover; simmer 45 minutes.

2 Stir in tofu, broccoli and parsley. Cook over medium heat about 10 minutes, stirring occasionally, until broccoli is crisp-tender.

tip for *two*

This is a very hearty, flavorful soup. If you haven't tried tofu lately, it's a terrific ingredient. If you'd rather make Lentil-Chicken Soup, just substitute 3/4 cup cut-up cooked chicken (about 4 oz) for the tofu.

1 Serving: Calories 270 (Calories from Fat 100); Total Fat 11g (Saturated Fat 1g; Trans Fat 0g); Cholesterol 0mg; Sodium 280mg; Total Carbohydrate 28g (Dietary Fiber 7g; Sugars 4g); Protein 15g   % Daily Value: Vitamin A 40%; Vitamin C 20%; Calcium 15%; Iron 30%   Exchanges: 1 1/2 Starch, 1 Vegetable, 1 Very Lean Meat, 2 Fat   Carbohydrate Choices: 2

Asian-Style Big Bowl Soup

Prep Time: 25 minutes | **Start to Finish:** 25 minutes | 2 servings

1/2 cup uncooked instant rice

1/2 cup water

1 teaspoon sesame or canola oil

1 clove garlic, finely chopped

2 medium green onions, chopped (2 tablespoons)

1 can (14 oz) chicken broth

1 medium carrot, cut into quarters lengthwise, then sliced (1/2 cup)

1 cup chopped cooked chicken breast

1/2 cup chopped bok choy or spinach

Dash pepper

1 Cook rice as directed on package, omitting butter and salt.

2 Meanwhile, in 2-quart nonstick saucepan, heat oil over medium-high heat. Cook garlic and onions in oil about 30 seconds, stirring frequently, until garlic is golden.

3 Increase heat to high. Stir in broth and carrot. Cover; heat to boiling, stirring occasionally.

4 Reduce heat to medium-low. Stir in chicken, bok choy and pepper. Cover; simmer 10 minutes to blend flavors.

5 To serve, place 1/2 cup cooked rice in each of 2 individual shallow soup plates. Ladle about 1 1/2 cups soup into each soup plate.

tip for *two*

This is one of the easiest soups you'll ever make. It's served in traditional Asian style. Vary the flavor by using turkey in place of the chicken.

1 Serving: Calories 290 (Calories from Fat 60); Total Fat 7g (Saturated Fat 1.5g; Trans Fat 0g); Cholesterol 55mg; Sodium 930mg; Total Carbohydrate 28g (Dietary Fiber 2g; Sugars 2g); Protein 28g **% Daily Value:** Vitamin A 90%; Vitamin C 10%; Calcium 6%; Iron 15% **Exchanges:** 2 Starch, 3 Very Lean Meat, 1 Fat **Carbohydrate Choices:** 2

Slow Cooker Tuscan Bean Soup

Prep Time: 15 minutes | **Start to Finish:** 8 hours 15 minutes | 4 servings (1 2/3 cups each); 2 servings for planned-overs

1 lb small red potatoes, cut into quarters (about 3 cups)

3 medium carrots, sliced (1 1/2 cups)

1 medium onion, chopped (1/2 cup)

2 cloves garlic, finely chopped

1 can (15 to 16 oz) great northern beans, drained, rinsed

1 can (14 oz) chicken broth

1 broth can (1 3/4 cups) water

1/2 cup diced cooked ham

1 1/2 teaspoons Italian seasoning

2 tablespoons chopped fresh parsley

1 tablespoon olive oil

1 In 3- to 3 1/2-quart slow cooker, mix all ingredients except parsley and oil.

2 Cover; cook on Low heat setting 8 to 10 hours.

3 Stir in parsley and oil.

tip for *two*

Whether you'll be at work, running errands or staying at home, just toss the ingredients in your slow cooker and let it do the work while you do your important tasks. This hearty soup begs to be served with whole-grain bread or rolls.

1 Serving: Calories 330 (Calories from Fat 50); Total Fat 6g (Saturated Fat 1.5g; Trans Fat 0g); Cholesterol 10mg; Sodium 720mg; Total Carbohydrate 51g (Dietary Fiber 10g; Sugars 5g); Protein 17g   **% Daily Value:** Vitamin A 110%; Vitamin C 15%; Calcium 15%; Iron 35%   **Exchanges:** 2 1/2 Starch, 1/2 Other Carbohydrate, 1 Vegetable, 1 Very Lean Meat, 1 Fat   **Carbohydrate Choices:** 3 1/2

Shrimp, Pepper and Rice Soup

Prep Time: 35 minutes | **Start to Finish:** 50 minutes | 2 servings (about 2 cups each)

1/2 cup uncooked brown rice

1 tablespoon butter (do not use margarine)

1 cup water

1/4 teaspoon seafood seasoning (from 6-oz container), if desired

2 tablespoons apple juice

1 small onion, chopped (1/4 cup)

1 clove garlic, finely chopped

1 1/2 cups reduced-sodium chicken broth

1/2 teaspoon dried thyme leaves

3/4 lb cooked deveined peeled large (21 to 26 count) shrimp, thawed if frozen, tail shells removed

1 medium red bell pepper, cut into strips

1 In 10-inch skillet, cook rice in butter over medium-high heat, stirring frequently, until rice is golden. Stir in water and seafood seasoning. Heat to boiling; reduce heat. Cover; simmer 30 to 35 minutes or until rice is almost tender and mixture is creamy.

2 Meanwhile, in 2-quart saucepan, cook apple juice, onion and garlic over medium-high heat 5 minutes, stirring frequently. Stir in remaining ingredients. Cook about 10 minutes, stirring occasionally, until hot.

3 Stir cooked rice into seafood mixture. Cook about 5 minutes, stirring occasionally, until rice is tender.

tip for *two*

The thyme adds an interesting herb flavor to this easy soup. If you'd rather use another dried herb, try marjoram or basil.

1 Serving: Calories 430 (Calories from Fat 80); Total Fat 9g (Saturated Fat 4.5g; Trans Fat 0g); Cholesterol 345mg; Sodium 850mg; Total Carbohydrate 44g (Dietary Fiber 7g; Sugars 5g); Protein 43g   **% Daily Value:** Vitamin A 50%; Vitamin C 100%; Calcium 10%; Iron 40%   **Exchanges:** 2 Starch, 1/2 Other Carbohydrate, 1 Vegetable, 5 Very Lean Meat, 1 Fat   **Carbohydrate Choices:** 3

Rustic Potato Soup
with Cheddar and Green Onions

Prep Time: 35 minutes | **Start to Finish:** 35 minutes | 2 servings (1 1/4 cups each)

1 1/2 cups water

1 lb unpeeled russet potatoes

1 cup fat-free (skim) milk

1 teaspoon butter or margarine

1/4 teaspoon salt

1/8 teaspoon pepper

8 medium green onions, finely chopped (1/2 cup)

1/2 cup shredded reduced-fat sharp Cheddar cheese (2 oz)

1 In 2-quart saucepan, heat water to boiling. Meanwhile, cut potatoes into 1/2-inch cubes; add to boiling water. Return to boiling; reduce heat. Cover; simmer 5 to 7 minutes or until tender.

2 Drain potatoes well; reserve 1 cup potatoes. Place remaining potatoes (about 1 1/2 cups) in blender. Add 1/2 cup of the milk. Cover; blend until smooth, adding additional milk if necessary. Return blended mixture to saucepan.

3 Add reserved 1 cup potatoes, remaining 1/2 cup milk, the butter, salt, pepper, 1/3 cup of the onions and 1/3 cup of the cheese to saucepan. Cook over medium heat 5 to 10 minutes, stirring frequently, until soup is hot and cheese is melted.

4 To serve, spoon soup into 2 soup bowls. Top with remaining onions and cheese.

tip for two

The potato adds not only great flavor, but it's also the thickener in this rustic soup, which is why part of it is blended. If you have a small food chopper or processor, you can use that instead of a blender.

1 Serving: Calories 290 (Calories from Fat 40); Total Fat 4.5g (Saturated Fat 2.5g; Trans Fat 0g); Cholesterol 15mg; Sodium 650mg; Total Carbohydrate 49g (Dietary Fiber 6g; Sugars 10g); Protein 15g **% Daily Value:** Vitamin A 15%; Vitamin C 25%; Calcium 45%; Iron 25% **Exchanges:** 2 Starch, 1 Other Carbohydrate, 1/2 Skim Milk, 1/2 Medium-Fat Meat **Carbohydrate Choices:** 3

Slow Cooker Split Pea and Ham Chowder

Prep Time: 10 minutes | **Start to Finish:** 6 hours 10 minutes | 4 servings (about 1 1/2 cups each); 2 servings for planned-overs

1 bag (1 lb) yellow split peas, sorted, rinsed

1 can (14 oz) reduced-sodium chicken broth

2 medium carrots, sliced (1 cup)

1 medium stalk celery, diced (1/2 cup)

2 cups water

3/4 cup diced cooked ham

1 teaspoon dried marjoram leaves

1 teaspoon onion powder

1/4 teaspoon salt

1/8 teaspoon red pepper sauce

1 In 3- to 3 1/2-quart slow cooker, mix all ingredients.

2 Cover; cook on Low heat setting 6 to 8 hours.

tip for *two*

What could be better than having dinner ready when you walk in the door? All it takes is assembling this easy soup before you leave in the morning. You can use green peas in place of the yellow ones.

1 Serving: Calories 420 (Calories from Fat 35); Total Fat 4g (Saturated Fat 1g; Trans Fat 0g); Cholesterol 15mg; Sodium 590mg; Total Carbohydrate 64g (Dietary Fiber 31g; Sugars 4g); Protein 31g   **% Daily Value:** Vitamin A 80%; Vitamin C 2%; Calcium 6%; Iron 25%   **Exchanges:** 4 Starch, 1 Vegetable, 2 1/2 Very Lean Meat   **Carbohydrate Choices:** 4

Caribbean Turkey Stew

Prep Time: 30 minutes | Start to Finish: 50 minutes | 2 servings (2 cups each)

2 teaspoons olive oil

1 small onion, coarsely chopped (1/4 cup)

1 clove garlic, finely chopped

1 turkey breast tenderloin (1/2 lb), cut into 1-inch pieces

1/4 teaspoon ground nutmeg

1/8 teaspoon pepper

1/2 dark-orange sweet potato, peeled, cut into 1-inch pieces (3/4 cup)

1 dried bay leaf

2 small red potatoes, cut into eighths (3/4 cup)

1 can (14 oz) chicken broth

1/2 cup frozen sweet peas (from 1-lb bag)

1. In 2-quart saucepan, heat oil over medium-high heat. Cook onion and garlic in oil 4 to 5 minutes, stirring frequently, until onion is softened.

2. Sprinkle turkey pieces with nutmeg and pepper. Stir into onion mixture. Cook 5 to 6 minutes, stirring occasionally, until turkey is no longer pink.

3. Stir in remaining ingredients except peas. Heat to boiling; reduce heat to medium-low. Cover; cook 18 to 20 minutes or until potatoes are tender.

4. Stir in frozen peas. Cover; cook 4 to 5 minutes, stirring occasionally, until peas are hot. Remove bay leaf.

tip for *two*

You can reduce the amount of sodium in any of the soups by using low-sodium broths instead of the regular ones.

1 Serving: Calories 300 (Calories from Fat 60); Total Fat 7g (Saturated Fat 1.5g; Trans Fat 0g); Cholesterol 75mg; Sodium 940mg; Total Carbohydrate 26g (Dietary Fiber 4g; Sugars 6g); Protein 34g   % Daily Value: Vitamin A 160%; Vitamin C 15%; Calcium 6%; Iron 20%   Exchanges: 1 1/2 Starch, 4 Very Lean Meat, 1 Fat   Carbohydrate Choices: 2

Teriyaki Beef Sandwiches

Prep Time: 20 minutes | **Start to Finish:** 20 minutes | 2 sandwiches

1/2 lb extra-lean (at least 90%) ground beef

1 tablespoon teriyaki marinade

2 tablespoons finely chopped water chestnuts

Dash pepper

2 medium green onions, finely chopped (2 tablespoons)

1 clove garlic, finely chopped

1 tablespoon teriyaki marinade

2 slices French bread (1/2 inch thick), toasted if desired

1/2 small bell pepper (any color), cut into rings

1 Heat closed medium-size contact grill for 5 to 10 minutes. In small bowl, mix beef, 1 tablespoon marinade, the water chestnuts, pepper, onions and garlic. Shape mixture into 2 patties, each about 3/4 inch thick.

2 Place patties on grill. Close grill. Grill 8 to 10 minutes, brushing with 1 tablespoon marinade, until meat thermometer inserted in center of patties reads 160°F.

3 Serve burgers on bread; top with bell pepper rings.

tip for *two*

Look for teriyaki marinade in the Asian-foods aisle of your grocery store. It's usually stocked with the bottles of soy sauce and hoisin sauce.

1 Sandwich: Calories 380 (Calories from Fat 100); Total Fat 11g (Saturated Fat 4g; Trans Fat 1g); Cholesterol 70mg; Sodium 830mg; Total Carbohydrate 41g (Dietary Fiber 2g; Sugars 6g); Protein 28g **% Daily Value:** Vitamin A 2%; Vitamin C 15%; Calcium 10%; Iron 30% **Exchanges:** 1 1/2 Starch, 1 Other Carbohydrate, 1 Vegetable, 3 Lean Meat, 1/2 Fat **Carbohydrate Choices:** 3

Bistro Beef Sandwiches

Prep Time: 25 minutes | **Start to Finish:** 25 minutes | 2 servings (2 sandwiches each)

4 frozen crusty French dinner rolls (from 12.4-oz bag)

1/4 cup water

1 teaspoon Worcestershire sauce

1 teaspoon cornstarch

1/8 teaspoon garlic salt

1 teaspoon olive oil

1/2 small onion, sliced, separated into rings

1/2 cup thin bite-size strips red, yellow and/or green bell pepper

2 slices (3/4 oz each) reduced-fat provolone cheese, quartered

4 thin slices (1 oz each) roast beef (from deli)

1 Heat dinner rolls as directed on package. Cool completely, about 10 minutes.

2 Meanwhile, in small bowl, stir together water, Worcestershire sauce, cornstarch and garlic salt; set aside.

3 In 10-inch skillet, heat oil over medium-high heat. Cook onion and bell pepper in oil 3 to 4 minutes, stirring occasionally, until vegetables are crisp-tender. Reduce heat to medium-low. Add cornstarch mixture; cook and stir until slightly thickened. Remove from heat.

4 Cut each roll in half crosswise with serrated knife. Place 2 cheese slice quarters on bottom half of each roll. Top each with 1 slice roast beef and 1/4 of the vegetable mixture; cover with top halves of rolls.

tip for *two*

Red or yellow bell pepper will provide a sweeter, more mild flavor than green bell pepper. Use the rest of the pepper in green salads or as a vegetable relish.

1 Serving: Calories 440 (Calories from Fat 160); Total Fat 17g (Saturated Fat 6g; Trans Fat 0g); Cholesterol 50mg; Sodium 610mg; Total Carbohydrate 42g (Dietary Fiber 0g; Sugars 6g); Protein 29g **% Daily Value:** Vitamin A 15%; Vitamin C 40%; Calcium 15%; Iron 25% **Exchanges:** 2 Starch, 1/2 Other Carbohydrate, 1 Vegetable, 3 Lean Meat, 1 1/2 Fat **Carbohydrate Choices:** 3

Broiled Dijon Burgers

Prep Time: 20 minutes | **Start to Finish:** 20 minutes | 2 sandwiches

1 egg or 2 egg whites

1 tablespoon fat-free (skim) milk

1 teaspoon Dijon mustard

1/8 teaspoon salt

1/8 teaspoon pepper

1/2 cup soft bread crumbs (about 1 slice bread)

2 tablespoons finely chopped onion

1/2 lb extra-lean (at least 90%) ground beef

2 whole-grain hamburger buns, split, toasted

1 Set oven control to broil. Spray broiler pan rack with cooking spray.

2 In small bowl, mix egg, milk, mustard, salt and pepper. Stir in bread crumbs and onion. Stir in beef. Shape mixture into 2 patties, each about 1/2 inch thick.

3 Place patties on rack in broiler pan. Broil with tops about 5 inches from heat about 10 minutes, turning once, until meat thermometer inserted in center of patties reads 160°F. Serve on buns.

tip for *two*

Use whole wheat bread for making the bread crumbs, and look for whole-grain hamburger buns. Top burgers with low-fat toppings, such as sliced tomatoes, sliced onion, pickles and mustard.

1 Sandwich: Calories 360 (Calories from Fat 130); Total Fat 14g (Saturated Fat 5g; Trans Fat 1g); Cholesterol 175mg; Sodium 610mg; Total Carbohydrate 28g (Dietary Fiber 3g; Sugars 6g); Protein 30g   **% Daily Value:** Vitamin A 4%; Vitamin C 0%; Calcium 8%; Iron 25%   **Exchanges:** 1 1/2 Starch, 1/2 Other Carbohydrate, 3 1/2 Lean Meat, 1/2 Fat Carbohydrate Choices: 2

Ham and Arugula Open-Face Sandwiches

Prep Time: 10 minutes | Start to Finish: 10 minutes | 2 sandwiches

2 tablespoons reduced-fat mayonnaise or salad dressing

1/2 teaspoon white wine vinegar or white vinegar

1/2 teaspoon prepared horse-radish

Dash pepper

2 slices whole-grain rye bread

1/4 lb thinly sliced cooked ham

1/4 cup firmly packed arugula or spinach leaves

2 radishes, sliced (2 tablespoons)

1 In small bowl, mix mayonnaise, vinegar, horseradish and pepper. Spread about 1 tablespoon mayonnaise mixture on each bread slice.

2 Layer ham and arugula alternately on bread. Top with radishes.

tip for *two*

This is a terrific sandwich for a light lunch, or team it with any of the soups in this chapter for a heartier lunch or dinner.

1 Sandwich: Calories 200 (Calories from Fat 80); Total Fat 9g (Saturated Fat 2g; Trans Fat 0g); Cholesterol 35mg; Sodium 960mg; Total Carbohydrate 15g (Dietary Fiber 1g; Sugars 3g); Protein 14g % Daily Value: Vitamin A 0%; Vitamin C 4%; Calcium 4%; Iron 10% Exchanges: 1 Starch, 1 1/2 Very Lean Meat, 1 1/2 Fat Carbohydrate Choices: 1

Everyone loves a bonus! Use these ideas to prepare a delicious first meal with the bonus of a head start on another.

1 Chicken-Veggies/Chicken-Veggie Melts

Marinate 4 chicken breast halves in herb-flavored marinade. Grill chicken with zucchini, red onion and bell pepper slices. Layer leftover chicken breasts and veggies on a slice of crusty bread. Top with salsa, tomato slices and shredded cheese.

2 Pork Tenderloin/Barbecue Pork Sandwiches

Bake and serve pork tenderloin slices. For the second meal, finely chop the remaining cooked pork, add barbecue sauce and heat. Fill 2 baked and split rolls with pork and diced red onion.

3 Ham Dinner/Ham Salad

Prepare a small boneless ham. For the second meal, finely chop leftover ham; mix with pickle relish and mayonnaise; split dinner rolls and fill with the ham mixture.

4 Turkey Tenderloins/Turkey Alfredo

Bake turkey breast tenderloins. For the second meal, make turkey Alfredo with white sauce from a dry mix, or heat Alfredo sauce from a jar. Cook linguine. Layer linguine, sauce and sliced turkey on plate; sprinkle grated Parmesan cheese over top.

5 Chicken Dinner/Asian Chicken Salad

Grill 4 chicken breast halves. Serve 2 with a vegetable and side dish, cube remaining cooked chicken; toss with mandarin orange segments, packaged salad greens and bottled Asian dressing. Sprinkle with chow mein noodles.

Grilled Italian Turkey Burgers

Prep Time: 30 minutes | Start to Finish: 30 minutes | 2 sandwiches

1/2 lb ground turkey breast

3 tablespoons tomato pasta sauce

1 tablespoon finely chopped red onion

2 slices (1 oz each) mozzarella cheese, cut in half

1/2 baguette (8 inches), cut into two 4-inch pieces

2 lettuce leaves

2 slices red onion

Additional tomato pasta sauce, if desired

1 Heat gas or charcoal grill. In medium bowl, mix turkey, 3 tablespoons pasta sauce and chopped onion. Shape mixture into 2 patties, each about 3/4 inch thick and the approximate shape of the baguette pieces.

2 Carefully brush grill rack with canola oil. Place patties on grill. Cover grill; cook over medium heat 12 to 15 minutes, turning once, until thermometer inserted in center of patties reads 165°F. Top patties with cheese. Cover grill; cook about 1 minute longer or until cheese is melted.

3 Cut baguette pieces in half horizontally. Place lettuce leaves on bottom halves; top with burgers and onion slices. Top with remaining baguette halves. Serve with additional pasta sauce.

tip for *two*

For any recipe that uses ground meat, you can use extra-lean ground beef, ground chicken or any ground meat. If you don't find 1/2 pound ground meat already packaged in the meat case, the butcher can usually weigh the amount you need.

1 Sandwich: Calories 450 (Calories from Fat 140); Total Fat 15g (Saturated Fat 6g; Trans Fat 1g); Cholesterol 90mg; Sodium 710mg; Total Carbohydrate 40g (Dietary Fiber 3g; Sugars 4g); Protein 38g   % Daily Value: Vitamin A 6%; Vitamin C 4%; Calcium 30%; Iron 20%   Exchanges: 2 Starch, 1/2 Other Carbohydrate, 4 1/2 Very Lean Meat, 2 1/2 Fat Carbohydrate Choices: 2 1/2

Grilled Stuffed Tuna Melts

Prep Time: 30 minutes | **Start to Finish:** 30 minutes | 2 sandwiches

1 can (6 oz) water-packed white tuna, drained

2 tablespoons finely chopped onion

2 tablespoons finely chopped green bell pepper

1 tablespoon finely chopped dill pickles

2 tablespoons creamy Dijon mustard-mayonnaise spread

1/4 cup shredded reduced-fat Cheddar cheese (1 oz)

4 slices whole-grain bread

1 Heat gas or charcoal grill for indirect-heat cooking as directed by manufacturer. Cut 2 (12 × 12-inch) sheets of heavy-duty foil. In small bowl, mix tuna, onion, bell pepper and pickles. Stir in mustard-mayonnaise spread and cheese.

2 Spoon tuna mixture onto 2 bread slices; add remaining bread slices. Place each sandwich on center of foil sheet. Bring up 2 sides of foil over sandwich so edges meet. Seal edges, making tight 1/2-inch fold; fold again, allowing space for heat circulation and expansion. Fold other sides to seal.

3 Place packets on grill for indirect cooking. Cover grill; cook 12 to 15 minutes, rotating packets 1/2 turn after 6 minutes, until sandwiches are thoroughly heated. To serve, cut large X across top of each packet; carefully fold back foil to allow steam to escape.

See photo on page 30

tip for *two*

Add crunch to your lunch! Serve carrot and celery sticks plus veggie chips with these sandwiches. These foil-wrapped sandwiches are grilled over indirect heat because using direct heat can cause the bread to burn quickly inside the foil.

1 Sandwich: Calories 280 (Calories from Fat 35); Total Fat 4g (Saturated Fat 1.5g; Trans Fat 0g); Cholesterol 25mg; Sodium 970mg; Total Carbohydrate 31g (Dietary Fiber 4g; Sugars 7g); Protein 29g **% Daily Value:** Vitamin A 2%; Vitamin C 6%; Calcium 15%; Iron 20% **Exchanges:** 1 1/2 Starch, 1/2 Other Carbohydrate, 3 1/2 Very Lean Meat **Carbohydrate Choices:** 2

Curried Chicken Sandwiches

Prep Time: 10 minutes | **Start to Finish:** 10 minutes | 2 sandwiches

2/3 cup diced cooked chicken

2 tablespoons reduced-fat mayonnaise or salad dressing

2 tablespoons sliced celery

1 tablespoon chopped peanuts

1 tablespoon chutney

1/2 teaspoon curry powder

2 lettuce leaves

4 slices raisin bread, toasted, if desired

1 In small bowl, mix all ingredients except lettuce and bread.

2 Place lettuce on 2 bread slices. Spoon about 1/2 cup chicken mixture onto each. Top with remaining bread.

tip for *two*

Any type of chutney works well in this tasty sandwich. In place of the celery, use any sliced or chopped fresh vegetable you have on hand.

1 Sandwich: Calories 320 (Calories from Fat 120); Total Fat 13g (Saturated Fat 2.5g; Trans Fat 0.5g); Cholesterol 45mg; Sodium 370mg; Total Carbohydrate 32g (Dietary Fiber 3g; Sugars 12g); Protein 19g **% Daily Value:** Vitamin A 2%; Vitamin C 2%; Calcium 6%; Iron 15% **Exchanges:** 2 Starch, 2 Lean Meat, 1 Fat **Carbohydrate Choices:** 2

Shrimp Salad Sandwiches

Prep Time: 10 minutes | **Start to Finish:** 10 minutes | 2 sandwiches

3 tablespoons reduced-fat mayonnaise or salad dressing

1 teaspoon soy sauce

1/2 teaspoon sugar

1/4 teaspoon ground ginger

1 can (4 to 4 1/2 oz) tiny shrimp, drained, rinsed

1 medium green onion, sliced (1 tablespoon)

2 teaspoons butter, softened (do not use margarine)

4 slices whole wheat bread

1/2 medium cucumber, thinly sliced (3/4 cup)

1 In small bowl, mix mayonnaise, soy sauce, sugar and ginger. Stir in shrimp and onion.

2 Spread butter on 1 side of 4 bread slices. Top 2 bread slices with cucumber slices. Spread about 1/3 cup shrimp mixture on cucumber slices; top with remaining bread.

tip for *two*

Take advantage of fish and seafood that come in small packages. Shrimp, crabmeat and tuna are available in smaller cans, perfect for two-person households.

1 Sandwich: Calories 330 (Calories from Fat 130); Total Fat 14g (Saturated Fat 4.5g; Trans Fat 0.5g); Cholesterol 130mg; Sodium 760mg; Total Carbohydrate 31g (Dietary Fiber 4g; Sugars 9g); Protein 18g   **% Daily Value:** Vitamin A 8%; Vitamin C 4%; Calcium 8%; Iron 20%   **Exchanges:** 2 Starch, 1 1/2 Very Lean Meat, 2 1/2 Fat   **Carbohydrate Choices:** 2

All-American Tuna Cakes

Prep Time: 25 minutes | **Start to Finish:** 25 minutes | 2 servings

1 can (6 oz) white tuna in water, drained, flaked

4 medium green onions, sliced (1/4 cup)

12 saltine crackers with unsalted tops, crushed (1/2 cup)

1 medium stalk celery, finely chopped (1/2 cup)

2 tablespoons reduced-fat mayonnaise or salad dressing

2 tablespoons chopped fresh parsley

1 tablespoon prepared horseradish

1 teaspoon Worcestershire sauce

1 egg or 2 egg whites, beaten

1/4 cup dry bread crumbs

1 tablespoon canola oil

1/4 cup fat-free tartar sauce

1 In small bowl, mix all ingredients except bread crumbs, oil and tartar sauce. Shape tuna mixture into 2 patties; coat evenly with bread crumbs.

2 In 10-inch nonstick skillet, heat oil over medium heat. Cook patties in oil about 6 minutes, turning once, until golden brown. Serve with tartar sauce.

tip for *two*

Pair these delicious tuna cakes with a few baby-cut carrots, cooked pea pods or a dark green romaine salad.

1 Serving: Calories 400 (Calories from Fat 170); Total Fat 19g (Saturated Fat 3g; Trans Fat 1g); Cholesterol 135mg; Sodium 890mg; Total Carbohydrate 32g (Dietary Fiber 2g; Sugars 8g); Protein 27g   **% Daily Value:** Vitamin A 15%; Vitamin C 8%; Calcium 8%; Iron 20%   **Exchanges:** 1 1/2 Starch, 1/2 Other Carbohydrate, 3 Lean Meat, 2 Fat Carbohydrate Choices: 2

Cheese and Bacon Sandwiches

Prep Time: 30 minutes | **Start to Finish:** 30 minutes | 2 sandwiches

4 slices bacon

2 slices red onion (1/4 inch thick)

2 slices (3/4 oz each) mozzarella cheese

4 slices sourdough or Vienna bread (1/2 inch thick)

1 Heat closed medium-size contact grill for 5 to 10 minutes. Place bacon on grill. Close grill. Grill 3 to 4 minutes or until browned. Removed bacon from grill; drain on paper towels. Cut bacon slices crosswise in half.

2 Carefully scrape most of drippings from grill into drip tray, using rubber scraper. Place onion on grill. Close grill. Grill 4 to 6 minutes or until tender.

3 To make sandwiches, layer bacon, onion and cheese between bread slices. Place sandwiches on grill. Close grill. Grill 3 to 5 minutes or until bread is toasted and cheese is melted.

tip for *two*

This tasty version of a classic comfort food can be tailored to please each of you when you use your favorite cheeses and breads.

1 Sandwich: Calories 350 (Calories from Fat 120); Total Fat 14g (Saturated Fat 6g; Trans Fat 0.5g); Cholesterol 30mg; Sodium 910mg; Total Carbohydrate 39g (Dietary Fiber 2g; Sugars 1g); Protein 18g   **% Daily Value:** Vitamin A 2%; Vitamin C 0%; Calcium 20%; Iron 15%   **Exchanges:** 2 1/2 Starch, 1 1/2 Medium-Fat Meat, 1 Fat   **Carbohydrate Choices:** 2 1/2

Classic Chicken Panini

Prep Time: 20 minutes | **Start to Finish:** 20 minutes | 2 sandwiches

2 boneless skinless chicken breasts

1/4 teaspoon salt-free seasoning blend

2 tablespoons reduced-fat mayonnaise or salad dressing

1 teaspoon white or flavored vinegar

1/4 teaspoon garlic powder

2 whole wheat English muffins, split

2 slices (3/4 oz each) mozzarella cheese

2 thin slices red onion

1/2 plum (Roma) tomato, cut into 4 slices

1 Heat closed medium-size contact grill for 5 to 10 minutes. Sprinkle chicken with seasoning blend. Place chicken on grill. Close grill; cook 4 to 5 minutes or until juice of chicken is clear when center of thickest part is cut (170°F).

2 Meanwhile, in small bowl, mix mayonnaise, vinegar and garlic powder. Spread on English muffin halves. Place chicken on bottoms of English muffins. Top with cheese, onion, tomato and tops of muffins.

3 Place sandwiches on grill. Close grill, pressing to flatten sandwiches; cook 2 to 3 minutes or until sandwiches are toasted.

tip for *two*

Regular tomatoes can take the place of the plum tomatoes, but they add more moisture to the sandwiches during grilling. Try other types of cheese, such as reduced-fat Swiss, provolone or Cheddar, in this sandwich.

1 Sandwich: Calories 410 (Calories from Fat 130); Total Fat 15g (Saturated Fat 5g; Trans Fat 0g); Cholesterol 90mg; Sodium 700mg; Total Carbohydrate 31g (Dietary Fiber 5g; Sugars 5g); Protein 38g **% Daily Value:** Vitamin A 6%; Vitamin C 0%; Calcium 35%; Iron 15% **Exchanges:** 1 1/2 Starch, 1/2 Other Carbohydrate, 5 Very Lean Meat, 2 Fat **Carbohydrate Choices:** 2

Garden-Fresh Greek Salad (page 60)

Simple Salads and Vegetables

Garden-Fresh Greek Salad

Prep Time: 20 minutes | **Start to Finish:** 20 minutes | 2 servings (1 1/3 cups each)

DRESSING

1 tablespoon lemon juice

1 teaspoon chopped fresh or
1/2 teaspoon dried oregano
leaves

1/4 teaspoon salt

1/4 teaspoon sugar

1/4 teaspoon Dijon mustard

Dash pepper

1 clove garlic, finely chopped

SALAD

2 cups ready-to-eat romaine
lettuce (from 10-oz bag)

1/4 cup chopped seeded peeled
cucumber

1/4 cup sliced red onion

2 tablespoons sliced kalamata
olives

1 medium tomato, seeded,
chopped (3/4 cup)

2 tablespoons reduced-fat feta
cheese

1 In small bowl, beat all dressing ingredients with wire whisk.

2 In medium bowl, toss all salad ingredients except cheese. Stir in dressing until salad is well coated. Sprinkle with cheese.

See photo on page 58

tip for *two*

Keep the meal Greek and low in fat by serving with grilled lamb chops plus pita wedges instead of bread.

1 Serving: Calories 70 (Calories from Fat 20); Total Fat 2.5g (Saturated Fat 1g; Trans Fat 0g); Cholesterol 0mg; Sodium 510mg; Total Carbohydrate 9g (Dietary Fiber 3g; Sugars 4g); Protein 4g   **% Daily Value:** Vitamin A 80%; Vitamin C 45%; Calcium 8%; Iron 6%   **Exchanges:** 2 Vegetable, 1/2 Fat   **Carbohydrate Choices:** 1/2

Citrus Pasta Salad with Rolls

Prep Time: 20 minutes | **Start to Finish:** 1 hour 20 minutes | 2 servings

1 box (9 oz) frozen cut broccoli

1/4 cup reduced-fat mayonnaise or salad dressing

1 teaspoon grated orange peel

1 tablespoon orange juice

1/4 teaspoon salt

3/4 cup cooked medium pasta shells

2 large radishes, sliced

1 orange, peeled, seeded and sectioned

2 frozen butterflake dinner rolls

1 Cook broccoli as directed on box. Remove cooked broccoli from pouch; rinse with cool water and drain well.

2 In 2-quart bowl, mix mayonnaise, orange peel, orange juice and salt. Stir in broccoli, pasta, radishes and orange. Cover; refrigerate at least 1 hour until chilled.

3 Bake dinner rolls as directed on package. Serve warm rolls with salad.

tip for *two*

If you like pasta dishes, cook extra when you make this salad, toss it with a drizzle of olive oil and refrigerate to use later.

1 Serving: Calories 410 (Calories from Fat 160); Total Fat 18g (Saturated Fat 3.5g; Trans Fat 2g); Cholesterol 10mg; Sodium 960mg; Total Carbohydrate 53g (Dietary Fiber 6g; Sugars 15g); Protein 11g   **% Daily Value:** Vitamin A 30%; Vitamin C 140%; Calcium 8%; Iron 15%   **Exchanges:** 3 Starch, 1 Vegetable, 3 Fat   **Carbohydrate Choices:** 3 1/2

Grilled Shrimp Louis Salad

Prep Time: 25 minutes | **Start to Finish:** 25 minutes | 2 servings

SALAD

1/2 lb uncooked deveined peeled medium (26 to 30 count) shrimp, thawed if frozen, tail shells removed

1 teaspoon olive oil

1/8 teaspoon salt

4 cups chopped romaine lettuce

1 medium stalk celery, finely chopped (1/2 cup)

1/2 cup chopped red bell pepper

1 cup grape tomatoes, cut in half

DRESSING

2 tablespoons reduced-fat mayonnaise or salad dressing

1 tablespoon plain reduced-fat yogurt

1 tablespoon shrimp cocktail sauce

1/2 teaspoon grated lemon peel

1/8 teaspoon salt

1 to 2 tablespoons fat-free (skim) milk

1 Heat gas or charcoal grill. On each of 2 (12-inch) metal skewers, thread shrimp, leaving 1/4-inch space between each shrimp. Brush with oil. Sprinkle with 1/8 teaspoon salt.

2 Place kabobs on grill. Cover grill; cook over medium heat 4 to 6 minutes, turning once, until shrimp are pink. Remove shrimp from skewers.

3 On 2 serving plates, place lettuce. Top with celery, bell pepper, tomatoes and grilled shrimp.

4 In small bowl, mix all dressing ingredients, adding enough milk for desired consistency. Spoon dressing onto centers of salads.

tip for *two*

Serving the dressing on the side allows each of you to use the amount you want.

1 Serving: Calories 220 (Calories from Fat 80); Total Fat 9g (Saturated Fat 1.5g; Trans Fat 0g); Cholesterol 165mg; Sodium 720mg; Total Carbohydrate 14g (Dietary Fiber 5g; Sugars 9g); Protein 21g   **% Daily Value:** Vitamin A 180%; Vitamin C 190%; Calcium 10%; Iron 25%   **Exchanges:** 1/2 Other Carbohydrate, 1 1/2 Vegetable, 2 1/2 Very Lean Meat, 1 1/2 Fat   **Carbohydrate Choices:** 1

Red Grapes and Shrimp Salad

Prep Time: 10 minutes | Start to Finish: 2 hours 10 minutes | 2 servings (1 cup shrimp mixture and 8 lettuce leaves each)

1/2 lb cooked deveined peeled medium (26 to 30 count) shrimp, thawed if frozen, tail shells removed

4 medium green onions, thinly sliced (1/4 cup)

2 tablespoons olive oil

1/4 teaspoon salt

1/8 teaspoon dried tarragon leaves

1 tablespoon red wine vinegar

Dash freshly ground pepper

1 cup seedless red grapes, cut in half

16 leaves leaf lettuce (about 3 cups)

1 In small bowl, place shrimp and onions. In tightly covered container, shake oil, salt, tarragon and vinegar; pour over shrimp. Sprinkle with pepper; toss until shrimp are well coated. Cover; refrigerate at least 2 hours.

2 Drain shrimp; reserve marinade to pour over salads if desired. Toss grapes with shrimp mixture. Serve on lettuce.

tip for *two*

Many interesting bakery breads would be great with this scrumptious salad. Try whole wheat sunflower bread or whole-grain rye.

1 Serving: Calories 310 (Calories from Fat 140); Total Fat 15g (Saturated Fat 2g; Trans Fat 0g); Cholesterol 220mg; Sodium 580mg; Total Carbohydrate 18g (Dietary Fiber 2g; Sugars 14g); Protein 26g   % Daily Value: Vitamin A 130%; Vitamin C 50%; Calcium 10%; Iron 25%   Exchanges: 1 Other Carbohydrate, 1 Vegetable, 3 1/2 Very Lean Meat, 2 1/2 Fat Carbohydrate Choices: 1

Marinated Shrimp Kabob Salad

Prep Time: 30 minutes | Start to Finish: 2 hours 30 minutes | 2 servings

1 1/2 teaspoons grated orange peel

1/4 cup orange juice

2 tablespoons canola oil

1/4 teaspoon crushed red pepper flakes

1/4 teaspoon salt

1 clove garlic, finely chopped

8 uncooked extra-large (16 to 20 count) shrimp (about 1/4 lb), thawed if frozen, peeled and deveined

4 pitted whole ripe olives (colossal size)

1/4 lb jicama, peeled, cut into 1-inch cubes (1 cup)

1/2 medium red bell pepper, cut into 1 1/2-inch pieces (1/2 cup)

1/4 small pineapple, cut into chunks (1 cup)

2 cups bite-size pieces salad greens

1 In small glass or plastic bowl, mix orange peel, orange juice, oil, red pepper flakes, salt and garlic; reserve half in second bowl to use as dressing. Stir shrimp into marinade in bowl. Cover; refrigerate at least 2 hours to marinate, but no longer than 6 hours.

2 Set oven control to broil. Remove shrimp from marinade; reserve marinade. On each of 4 (11-inch) metal skewers, alternate 2 shrimp, 1 olive and pieces of jicama, bell pepper and pineapple. Place on rack in broiler pan.

3 Broil kabobs with tops about 4 inches from heat about 8 minutes, turning and brushing once with reserved marinade, until shrimp are pink.

4 Divide greens between 2 plates. Top each plate with 2 kabobs; remove skewers. Serve with reserved dressing.

tip for *two*
These colorful kabobs are perfect served over a bed of whole wheat couscous or brown rice.

1 Serving: Calories 240 (Calories from Fat 100); Total Fat 11g (Saturated Fat 1g; Trans Fat 0g); Cholesterol 80mg; Sodium 440mg; Total Carbohydrate 24g (Dietary Fiber 7g; Sugars 13g); Protein 11g   **% Daily Value:** Vitamin A 80%; Vitamin C 90%; Calcium 8%; Iron 20%   **Exchanges:** 1 Other Carbohydrate, 1 1/2 Vegetable, 1 Very Lean Meat, 2 Fat **Carbohydrate Choices:** 1 1/2

Tropical Salsa-Topped Chicken Salad

Prep Time: 15 minutes | **Start to Finish:** 30 minutes | 2 servings

2 cups (4 oz each) tropical fruit in lightly sweetened juice (from 16-oz package)

1 teaspoon grated lime peel

1/4 teaspoon salt

2 boneless skinless chicken breasts, cut into 1-inch pieces

1/2 medium red bell pepper, chopped (1/2 cup)

2 medium green onions, sliced (2 tablespoons)

1 tablespoon finely chopped fresh cilantro

1 bag (6 oz) fresh baby spinach leaves

1 tablespoon flaked coconut

1 Drain fruit cups, reserving juice. In small bowl, mix 2 tablespoons reserved juice, the lime peel and salt. Add chicken pieces; toss to coat. Cover; refrigerate 15 minutes, stirring once.

2 Meanwhile, in medium bowl, mix drained fruit, bell pepper, onions and cilantro; set aside.

3 Heat 10-inch nonstick skillet over medium-low heat. Add chicken with marinade. Cook 6 to 8 minutes, stirring frequently, until chicken is brown on outside and no longer pink in center.

4 In large bowl, toss spinach with remaining reserved juice. On 2 dinner plates, arrange spinach. Top with chicken and fruit mixture. Sprinkle with coconut.

tip for two

Buy the tropical fruit in the canned fruit aisle at your grocery store. These individual cups of fruit come in packages of four.

1 Serving: Calories 310 (Calories from Fat 50); Total Fat 5g (Saturated Fat 2g; Trans Fat 0g); Cholesterol 75mg; Sodium 450mg; Total Carbohydrate 35g (Dietary Fiber 5g; Sugars 22g); Protein 31g **% Daily Value:** Vitamin A 200%; Vitamin C 90%; Calcium 15%; Iron 20% **Exchanges:** 2 Other Carbohydrate, 1 Vegetable, 4 Very Lean Meat, 1/2 Fat **Carbohydrate Choices:** 2

Chicken-Fruit Salad

Prep Time: 10 minutes | **Start to Finish:** 40 minutes | 2 servings

1/3 cup plain reduced-fat yogurt

2 tablespoons reduced-fat mayonnaise or salad dressing

1 cup cubed cooked chicken breast

2/3 cup seedless green grapes

1 large peach, chopped (3/4 cup)

1 medium stalk celery, diced (1/2 cup)

1 teaspoon chopped fresh or 1/2 teaspoon dried mint leaves

1 In medium bowl, mix yogurt and mayonnaise until smooth. Stir in remaining ingredients.

2 Cover; refrigerate at least 30 minutes until chilled.

tip for two

Make it special by placing Bibb lettuce leaves in the salad bowls before serving this fresh salad. Bake two frozen crusty dinner rolls while the salad chills.

1 Serving: Calories 260 (Calories from Fat 80); Total Fat 9g (Saturated Fat 2g; Trans Fat 0g); Cholesterol 65mg; Sodium 200mg; Total Carbohydrate 21g (Dietary Fiber 2g; Sugars 17g); Protein 24g   **% Daily Value:** Vitamin A 10%; Vitamin C 20%; Calcium 10%; Iron 6%   **Exchanges:** 1/2 Fruit, 1 Other Carbohydrate, 3 1/2 Very Lean Meat, 1 Fat **Carbohydrate Choices:** 1 1/2

Marinated Broccoli and Carrot Salad

Prep Time: 20 minutes | **Start to Finish:** 1 hour 20 minutes | 2 servings

1 1/2 cups broccoli florets

1/4 cup sliced carrot

1 medium green onion, sliced
(1 tablespoon)

3 tablespoons low-fat Italian
dressing

2 lettuce leaves

1 In 1 1/2-quart saucepan, heat 1 inch water to boiling. Add broccoli, carrot and onion. Cover; heat to boiling. Reduce heat. Boil 10 to 12 minutes or until broccoli is crisp-tender; drain.

2 Toss vegetables with dressing. Cover; refrigerate about 1 hour or until chilled. Serve on lettuce leaves.

tip for *two*

Add a splash of color and extra nutrients by cooking 1/4 cup chopped red bell pepper with the other vegetables.

1 Serving: Calories 70 (Calories from Fat 40); Total Fat 4.5g (Saturated Fat 0.5g; Trans Fat 0g); Cholesterol 0mg; Sodium 320mg; Total Carbohydrate 7g (Dietary Fiber 2g; Sugars 3g); Protein 2g **% Daily Value:** Vitamin A 60%; Vitamin C 45%; Calcium 4%; Iron 4% **Exchanges:** 1 Vegetable, 1 Fat **Carbohydrate Choices:** 1/2

Blue Cheese Waldorf Salad

Prep Time: 10 minutes | **Start to Finish:** 1 hour 10 minutes | 2 servings

3 tablespoons plain reduced-fat yogurt

2 teaspoons reduced-fat mayonnaise or salad dressing

1 tablespoon finely crumbled blue cheese

2 medium unpeeled red eating apples, cut into 1/4-inch slices

Lemon juice

1 cup tightly packed spinach leaves

1 medium stalk celery, thinly sliced (1/2 cup)

1 tablespoon chopped walnuts, toasted

1 In small bowl, mix yogurt, mayonnaise and blue cheese. Cover; refrigerate at least 1 hour to blend flavors.

2 Sprinkle apple slices with lemon juice to prevent browning. In large bowl, toss apples and spinach. Spoon blue cheese mixture over salad. Sprinkle with celery and walnuts.

tip for two

You can toast nuts ahead of time. Bake uncovered in an ungreased shallow pan in a 350°F oven 6 to 10 minutes, stirring occasionally, until nuts are light brown. Or cook in an ungreased heavy skillet over medium heat 5 to 7 minutes, stirring frequently until nuts begin to brown.

1 Serving: Calories 160 (Calories from Fat 50); Total Fat 6g (Saturated Fat 1.5g; Trans Fat 0g); Cholesterol 5mg; Sodium 140mg; Total Carbohydrate 23g (Dietary Fiber 4g; Sugars 16g); Protein 4g **% Daily Value:** Vitamin A 35%; Vitamin C 20%; Calcium 10%; Iron 4% **Exchanges:** 1 Fruit, 1 Vegetable, 1 1/2 Fat **Carbohydrate Choices:** 1 1/2

Sweet-and-Sour Cabbage Slaw

Prep Time: 5 minutes | **Start to Finish:** 5 minutes | 2 servings

2 tablespoons honey

2 tablespoons peach or apricot spreadable fruit

2 teaspoons cider vinegar

2 cups coleslaw mix or shredded cabbage

1 medium carrot, shredded (2/3 cup)

2 medium green onions, sliced (2 tablespoons)

1 In medium bowl, mix honey, spreadable fruit and vinegar.

2 Add remaining ingredients; toss.

tip for *two*

Chill this tasty side for 30 minutes to blend flavors while you prepare grilled pork chops or chicken.

1 Serving: Calories 160 (Calories from Fat 0); Total Fat 0g (Saturated Fat 0g; Trans Fat 0g); Cholesterol 0mg; Sodium 40mg; Total Carbohydrate 38g (Dietary Fiber 4g; Sugars 32g); Protein 2g   **% Daily Value:** Vitamin A 90%; Vitamin C 45%; Calcium 6%; Iron 6%   **Exchanges:** 2 Other Carbohydrate, 1 Vegetable   **Carbohydrate Choices:** 2 1/2

Fresh Tomato and Cucumber Salad

Prep Time: 10 minutes | Start to Finish: 15 minutes | 2 servings

1 medium tomato, cut into 6 slices

1/2 cup chopped cucumber

1/8 teaspoon salt

1 1/2 teaspoons finely chopped fresh basil leaves

1 teaspoon grated lemon peel

1 teaspoon sugar

1 tablespoon balsamic vinegar

1 On 2 salad plates, arrange tomato slices in a circle, slightly overlapping. Top with cucumber. Sprinkle salt over tomatoes and cucumber.

2 In small bowl, mix basil, lemon peel and sugar; sprinkle over salads. Drizzle with vinegar. Let stand 5 minutes before serving.

tip for *two*

If you prefer parsley, use it in place of the basil.

1 **Serving:** Calories 30 (Calories from Fat 0); Total Fat 0g (Saturated Fat 0g; Trans Fat 0g); Cholesterol 0mg; Sodium 150mg; Total Carbohydrate 6g (Dietary Fiber 1g; Sugars 5g); Protein 0g   **% Daily Value:** Vitamin A 10%; Vitamin C 15%; Calcium 0%; Iron 0%   **Exchanges:** 1 Vegetable   **Carbohydrate Choices:** 1/2

Broccoli, Feta and Tomato Salad

Prep Time: 10 minutes | **Start to Finish:** 10 minutes | 2 servings (about 1/2 cup each)

2 cups water

1 cup fresh broccoli florets

1 small plum (Roma) tomato, chopped (1/3 cup)

2 tablespoons reduced-fat feta cheese

1 tablespoon fat-free balsamic vinaigrette

1 teaspoon chopped fresh or 1/2 teaspoon dried oregano leaves

1 In 1-quart saucepan, heat water to boiling over high heat. Add broccoli; cook 10 to 20 seconds or until broccoli is bright green. Drain broccoli; rinse in cold water until cool.

2 In small serving bowl, stir broccoli and remaining ingredients.

tip for *two*

Cooking the broccoli for a very short time, called blanching, brings out the bright green color and softens it just a bit for this salad. Chopped red onion and diced red bell pepper are nice additions to this salad.

1 Serving: Calories 45 (Calories from Fat 10); Total Fat 1.5g (Saturated Fat 1g; Trans Fat 0g); Cholesterol 0mg; Sodium 250mg; Total Carbohydrate 5g (Dietary Fiber 2g; Sugars 2g); Protein 3g **% Daily Value:** Vitamin A 10%; Vitamin C 60%; Calcium 4%; Iron 2% **Exchanges:** 1 Vegetable, 1/2 Fat **Carbohydrate Choices:** 1/2

Wilted Spinach Salad

Prep Time: 20 minutes | **Start to Finish:** 20 minutes | 2 servings (about 1 1/2 cups each)

SALAD

4 cups bite-size pieces spinach (4 oz)

1/4 cup shredded mozzarella cheese (1 oz)

1 hard-cooked egg, chopped

1/2 medium red bell pepper, cut into bite-size strips (1/2 cup)

HOT VINAIGRETTE

1 teaspoon canola oil

1 small onion, finely chopped (1/4 cup)

1 teaspoon sugar

1/4 teaspoon ground mustard

1/4 cup cider vinegar

1 In medium bowl, toss all salad ingredients.

2 In 8-inch skillet, heat oil over medium heat. Cook onion in oil about 1 minute, stirring occasionally, until tender. Stir in sugar and mustard. Gradually stir in vinegar. Heat until hot.

3 Immediately pour vinaigrette over salad; toss. Serve immediately.

tip for *two*

If you have canned cannellini, kidney or garbanzo beans left over from another recipe, sprinkle a few over the top of this side salad. They will add flavor and fiber to the mix.

1 Serving: Calories 150 (Calories from Fat 70); Total Fat 8g (Saturated Fat 3g; Trans Fat 0g); Cholesterol 115mg; Sodium 150mg; Total Carbohydrate 10g (Dietary Fiber 2g; Sugars 6g); Protein 9g   **% Daily Value:** Vitamin A 130%; Vitamin C 100%; Calcium 20%; Iron 15%   **Exchanges:** 2 Vegetable, 1 Medium-Fat Meat, 1/2 Fat   **Carbohydrate Choices:** 1/2

Asparagus Parmesan

Prep Time: 10 minutes | **Start to Finish:** 10 minutes | 2 servings (1 cup each)

1 box (9 oz) Green Giant® frozen asparagus cuts

1 cup sliced fresh mushrooms

2 teaspoons butter (do not use margarine)

1/8 teaspoon garlic powder

Freshly ground pepper

1 tablespoon grated Parmesan cheese

1 Remove asparagus from pouch; place in medium microwavable bowl. Microwave on High 2 minutes.

2 Stir in remaining ingredients except Parmesan cheese. Microwave 2 to 4 minutes longer, stirring occasionally, until asparagus is crisp-tender and thoroughly heated. Sprinkle with Parmesan cheese just before serving.

tip for *two*

If you're short on time or don't have fresh mushrooms on hand, use a 2.5-ounce jar of sliced mushrooms instead. Top this tasty side with shredded fresh Parmesan cheese, if you like, instead of the grated cheese.

1 Serving: Calories 90 (Calories from Fat 50); Total Fat 5g (Saturated Fat 3g; Trans Fat 0g); Cholesterol 15mg; Sodium 90mg; Total Carbohydrate 4g (Dietary Fiber 2g; Sugars 3g); Protein 6g **% Daily Value:** Vitamin A 20%; Vitamin C 25%; Calcium 6%; Iron 4% **Exchanges:** 1 Vegetable, 1/2 Lean Meat, 1/2 Fat **Carbohydrate Choices:** 0

Grilled Baby Carrots and Green Beans

Prep Time: 35 minutes | **Start to Finish:** 35 minutes | 2 servings

1/2 cup ready-to-eat baby-cut carrots, cut in half lengthwise

4 oz fresh green beans (1 cup)

1 1/2 teaspoons olive oil

1/4 teaspoon dried marjoram leaves

1/4 teaspoon garlic-pepper blend

Dash salt

1/2 medium red onion, cut into 1/2-inch wedges

1 Heat gas or charcoal grill. In medium bowl, toss all ingredients except onion. Place in grill basket (grill "wok"). Reserve oil mixture in bowl.

2 Place grill basket on grill. Cover grill; cook over medium heat 10 minutes.

3 Add onion to oil mixture in bowl; toss to coat. Add onion to grill basket. Cover grill; cook 8 to 10 minutes longer, shaking basket or stirring vegetables occasionally, until all vegetables are crisp-tender.

tip for *two*

Clean up your grill basket quickly by soaking it in warm water immediately after you remove it from the grill.

1 Serving: Calories 70 (Calories from Fat 30); Total Fat 3.5g (Saturated Fat 0.5g; Trans Fat 0g); Cholesterol 0mg; Sodium 100mg; Total Carbohydrate 9g (Dietary Fiber 3g; Sugars 4g); Protein 1g   **% Daily Value:** Vitamin A 80%; Vitamin C 4%; Calcium 4%; Iron 4%   **Exchanges:** 1 Vegetable, 1 Fat   **Carbohydrate Choices:** 1/2

1 Roasted Vegetable–Pasta Salad

Buy deli-roasted vegetables. Cook fresh refrigerated pasta or dried pasta from your pantry, like cavatappi, fusilli or another fun shape. Toss pasta and veggies.

2 Asian Noodle–Chicken Salad

Buy 1 or 2 cooked chicken breasts. Slice chicken; toss with deli Asian noodles. Sprinkle with toasted sesame seed. Serve warm or cold.

3 Spinach-Pasta Salad

Add a little milk to purchased spinach dip so the dip has a dressing-like consistency; toss with cooked pasta. Add chopped leftover vegetables if desired.

4 Hummus-Vegetable Sandwiches

Spread purchased hummus in pockets of halved whole wheat pita bread. Fill with deli-roasted vegetables.

5 Southwest Tortilla Roll-Ups

Spread purchased Southwest dip on whole wheat tortillas. Sprinkle with shredded rotisserie chicken and shredded cheese; roll up.

5 *easy* Deli Fix-Ups for Two

Keep your lunches, dinners and sides easy and full of variety by starting with a purchased deli item:

Grilled Cheesy Garlic Potato Packet

Prep Time: 30 minutes | **Start to Finish:** 30 minutes | 2 servings

1/2 teaspoon olive oil

1 Yukon Gold potato (8 oz), cut into 1/2-inch pieces

2 teaspoons fresh chopped chives

1/2 teaspoon garlic salt

1 tablespoon grated Parmesan cheese

1 Heat gas or charcoal grill. Cut 1 (14 × 12-inch) sheet of heavy-duty foil. Spray one side generously with cooking spray.

2 In small bowl, pour oil over potato pieces; toss to coat. Add chives and garlic salt; toss to coat. Sprinkle with cheese; toss to coat.

3 Place potatoes on center of foil sheet. Bring up 2 sides of foil so edges meet. Seal edges, making tight 1/2-inch fold; fold again, allowing space for heat circulation and expansion. Fold other sides to seal.

4 Place packet on grill. Cover grill; cook over medium low heat 15 to 20 minutes, rotating packet 1/2 turn after 8 minutes, until potatoes are golden brown and tender.

tip for *two*

When you have your grill fired up to make steak or chicken, toss these delicious potatoes alongside your meat for grilling. Sprinkle potatoes with coarsely ground pepper right before serving.

1 Serving: Calories 110 (Calories from Fat 20); Total Fat 2g (Saturated Fat 1g; Trans Fat 0g); Cholesterol 0mg; Sodium 310mg; Total Carbohydrate 20g (Dietary Fiber 3g; Sugars 1g); Protein 3g **% Daily Value:** Vitamin A 0%; Vitamin C 10%; Calcium 6%; Iron 10% **Exchanges:** 1 Starch, 1/2 Fat **Carbohydrate Choices:** 1

Lentil-Corn Pilaf

Prep Time: 10 minutes | **Start to Finish:** 30 minutes | 2 servings (1/2 cup each)

1/2 cup water

1/4 cup dried lentils (2 oz), sorted, rinsed

2 tablespoons chopped red bell pepper

1/4 cup frozen (thawed) or canned (drained) whole kernel corn

2 teaspoons chopped fresh cilantro or parsley

1/8 teaspoon chili powder

1/8 teaspoon salt

1 In 1-quart saucepan, heat water to boiling. Stir in lentils and bell pepper; reduce heat. Cover; simmer 15 to 20 minutes or until lentils are tender. Drain if necessary.

2 Stir in remaining ingredients. Cook over low heat 2 to 3 minutes, stirring occasionally, until corn is tender and hot.

tip for *two*

For more south-of-the-border spice, chop a jalapeño chile and add with the red bell pepper. This fiber-rich pilaf makes a terrific accompaniment to grilled chops or baked chicken.

1 Serving: Calories 100 (Calories from Fat 0); Total Fat 0g (Saturated Fat 0g; Trans Fat 0g); Cholesterol 0mg; Sodium 150mg; Total Carbohydrate 18g (Dietary Fiber 5g; Sugars 1g); Protein 7g   **% Daily Value:** Vitamin A 8%; Vitamin C 15%; Calcium 0%; Iron 15%   **Exchanges:** 1 Starch, 1/2 Very Lean Meat   **Carbohydrate Choices:** 1

Scalloped Corn

Prep Time: 20 minutes | **Start to Finish:** 35 minutes | 2 servings (1/2 cup each)

1 teaspoon butter (do not use margarine)

2 tablespoons finely chopped onion

2 tablespoons finely chopped green bell pepper

2 teaspoons all-purpose flour

1/4 teaspoon salt

1/8 teaspoon ground mustard

Dash pepper

1/3 cup fat-free (skim) milk

1 cup frozen whole kernel corn (from 1-lb bag), thawed

1/2 cup Country® Corn Flakes cereal

2 teaspoons butter, melted (do not use margarine)

1 Heat oven to 350°F. In 8-inch nonstick skillet, melt 1 teaspoon butter over medium heat. Cook onion and bell pepper in butter 2 to 4 minutes, stirring occasionally, until crisp-tender.

2 Stir in flour, salt, mustard and pepper. Cook 1 to 2 minutes, stirring constantly, until smooth and well mixed; remove from heat.

3 Stir in milk. Heat to boiling, stirring constantly; boil and stir 1 minute. Stir in corn. Divide between 2 ungreased 8-ounce custard cups.

4 In small bowl, mix cereal and 2 teaspoons melted butter; sprinkle over corn mixture. Bake uncovered 10 to 15 minutes or until mixture is bubbly and topping is golden.

tip for *two*

For a homey southern meal, serve this corn casserole with a ham steak or fried chicken, and add coleslaw and biscuits.

1 Serving: Calories 180 (Calories from Fat 60); Total Fat 7g (Saturated Fat 4g; Trans Fat 0g); Cholesterol 15mg; Sodium 420mg; Total Carbohydrate 27g (Dietary Fiber 2g; Sugars 6g); Protein 4g   **% Daily Value:** Vitamin A 10%; Vitamin C 10%; Calcium 10%; Iron 15%   **Exchanges:** 1 Starch, 1 Other Carbohydrate, 1 Fat   **Carbohydrate Choices:** 2

Broccoli and Carrots with Creamy Parmesan Sauce

Prep Time: 20 minutes | **Start to Finish:** 20 minutes | 2 servings (1 cup vegetables and 2 tablespoons sauce each)

1 cup ready-to-eat baby-cut carrots

1/4 lb broccoli, cut into florets and stems (1 cup)

1 tablespoon (3/4 oz) reduced-fat cream cheese (Neufchâtel)

2 tablespoons fat-free (skim) milk

1 teaspoon butter (do not use margarine)

1 tablespoon grated Parmesan cheese

1 teaspoon chopped fresh chives

1 In 2-quart saucepan, heat 1 inch water to boiling. Add carrots; heat to boiling. Boil about 5 minutes or until crisp-tender. Add broccoli; boil 2 minutes longer. Drain; keep warm.

2 Meanwhile, in 1-quart saucepan, cook cream cheese, milk and butter over medium heat, stirring constantly, until smooth and thoroughly heated. Remove from heat. Stir in Parmesan cheese.

3 Sprinkle chives over sauce. Serve with vegetables.

tip for *two*

Just a bit of sauce adds terrific flavor to this broccoli and carrot side dish.

1 Serving: Calories 110 (Calories from Fat 50); Total Fat 6g (Saturated Fat 3.5g; Trans Fat 0g); Cholesterol 15mg; Sodium 180mg; Total Carbohydrate 10g (Dietary Fiber 3g; Sugars 5g); Protein 5g   **% Daily Value:** Vitamin A 160%; Vitamin C 35%; Calcium 10%; Iron 4%   **Exchanges:** 2 Vegetable, 1 Fat   **Carbohydrate Choices:** 1/2

Oven-Roasted Sweet Potato

Prep Time: 10 minutes | **Start to Finish:** 45 minutes | 2 servings (3/4 cup each)

1 small dark-orange sweet potato, peeled, cut into 1-inch chunks (1 cup)

1 medium onion, cut crosswise in half, then cut into wedges

3 tablespoons reduced-fat Italian dressing

Dash ground red pepper (cayenne)

1/2 medium red or green bell pepper, cut into 1-inch squares (1/2 cup)

1 Move oven rack to position slightly above middle of oven. Heat oven to 500°F.

2 Generously spray 8-inch square pan with cooking spray. Place sweet potato and onion in pan. Mix dressing and ground red pepper; pour over vegetables.

3 Cover with foil. Roast 20 minutes. Stir in bell pepper. Cover; roast 5 minutes. Stir vegetables; roast uncovered 10 minutes longer.

tip for *two*

For a healthy diet, experts recommend eating five to nine servings of fruits and vegetables every day. This tasty sweet potato and pepper dish makes it easy to eat more vegetables.

1 Serving: Calories 120 (Calories from Fat 40); Total Fat 4.5g (Saturated Fat 0.5g; Trans Fat 0g); Cholesterol 0mg; Sodium 310mg; Total Carbohydrate 19g (Dietary Fiber 3g; Sugars 9g); Protein 2g **% Daily Value:** Vitamin A 210%; Vitamin C 50%; Calcium 4%; Iron 4% **Exchanges:** 1 Starch, 1 Fat **Carbohydrate Choices:** 1

Mediterranean Grilled Snapper (page 89)

Easy Main Dishes

Baked Sea Bass

Prep Time: 15 minutes | **Start to Finish:** 30 minutes | 2 servings

2 teaspoons butter (do not use margarine)

1 medium leek, finely chopped (1/2 cup)

3/4 lb sea bass fillets, skin removed, cut into 2 serving pieces

1 tablespoon chopped fresh parsley

1/2 teaspoon dried thyme leaves

1/8 teaspoon salt

1/8 teaspoon pepper

1 tablespoon dry white wine or nonalcoholic wine

1 tablespoon butter (do not use margarine)

1 Heat oven to 350°F. In 8-inch skillet, melt 2 teaspoons butter over medium heat. Cook leek in butter, stirring occasionally, until soft, about 5 minutes.

2 In bottom of 8-inch square (2-quart) glass baking dish, arrange leek. Place fish on leek; top with remaining ingredients except 1 tablespoon butter.

3 Cover with foil. Bake 10 to 15 minutes or until fish flakes easily with fork. Using slotted spoon, remove fish, leek and herbs from pan; arrange on serving platter and keep warm.

4 Simmer remaining liquid in pan over low heat. Add 1 tablespoon butter, a little at a time, beating constantly with wire whisk until mixture is slightly thickened. Pour sauce over fish and herbs.

tip for *two*

For overall good health, aim to eat fish at least once a week. With this easy and great-tasting recipe, that goal won't be hard to achieve. You can use green onions in place of the leek, if you prefer.

1 Serving: Calories 290 (Calories from Fat 150); Total Fat 16g (Saturated Fat 8g; Trans Fat 0.5g); Cholesterol 110mg; Sodium 320mg; Total Carbohydrate 4g (Dietary Fiber 0g; Sugars 0g); Protein 33g   **% Daily Value:** Vitamin A 20%; Vitamin C 6%; Calcium 6%; Iron 15%   **Exchanges:** 1 Vegetable, 4 1/2 Lean Meat, 1/2 Fat   **Carbohydrate Choices:** 0

Mediterranean Grilled Snapper

Prep Time: 15 minutes | **Start to Finish:** 2 hours 30 minutes | 2 servings

3/4 lb red snapper fillets, cut into 2 serving pieces

1 tablespoon olive oil

2 tablespoons lemon juice

2 tablespoons chopped fresh basil

1 tablespoon chopped fresh rosemary

1 clove garlic, finely chopped

2 tablespoons chopped ripe olives

1/2 small zucchini, sliced (1/2 cup)

1/2 small tomato, chopped (1/4 cup)

1 In 8-inch square (2-quart) glass baking dish, place fish. In small bowl, mix oil, lemon juice, basil, rosemary and garlic; pour over fish. Cover; refrigerate 2 hours to marinate.

2 Remove fish from marinade; set aside. Pour marinade into 1-quart saucepan. Add olives, zucchini and tomato to marinade. Cook over medium heat 4 to 5 minutes, stirring occasionally, until zucchini is crisp-tender.

3 Heat gas or charcoal grill. Carefully brush grill rack with canola oil. Place fish, skin sides down, on grill. Cover grill; cook over medium heat 10 to 15 minutes or until fish flakes easily with fork. Spoon tomato olive mixture over snapper.

BROILING DIRECTIONS: Marinate fish as directed. Set oven control to broil. Brush broiler pan rack with oil; place fish on rack in pan. Broil with tops about 4 inches from heat 10 to 15 minutes or until fish flakes easily with fork.

See photo on page 86

tip for *two*

Olive oil is a good oil to use for savory recipes because it is high in monounsaturated fat, a good fat for your heart and your health.

1 Serving: Calories 240 (Calories from Fat 90); Total Fat 10g (Saturated Fat 1.5g; Trans Fat 0g); Cholesterol 90mg; Sodium 220mg; Total Carbohydrate 4g (Dietary Fiber 1g; Sugars 1g); Protein 33g   **% Daily Value:** Vitamin A 10%; Vitamin C 10%; Calcium 4%; Iron 6%   **Exchanges:** 1 Vegetable, 4 1/2 Very Lean Meat, 1 1/2 Fat   **Carbohydrate Choices:** 0

Butterfly Shrimp

Prep Time: 20 minutes | **Start to Finish:** 1 hour 20 minutes | 2 servings

1/2 lb uncooked fresh extra-large (16 to 20 count) shrimp

1/4 cup dry white wine or nonalcoholic wine

1 tablespoon chopped fresh parsley

2 teaspoons canola oil

1/2 teaspoon dried basil leaves

1/8 teaspoon salt

2 lemon wedges

1 Peel shrimp. Make shallow cut lengthwise down back of each shrimp; wash out vein. Press each shrimp flat into butterfly shape. Place shrimp in small glass or plastic bowl.

2 In another small bowl, mix remaining ingredients except lemon; pour over shrimp. Cover; refrigerate at least 1 hour to marinate.

3 Set oven control to broil. Lightly brush broiler pan rack with oil. Remove shrimp from marinade; reserve marinade. Place shrimp on rack in broiler pan.

4 Broil shrimp with tops about 4 inches from heat about 5 minutes, turning and brushing once with reserved marinade, until shrimp are pink. Garnish with lemon wedges and, if desired, additional chopped fresh parsley.

tip for *two*

Canola oil is an excellent oil to use for sautéing, stir-frying and baking. Because it is very high in monounsaturated fat, it may help lower blood cholesterol and triglycerides (fats found in blood).

1 Serving: Calories 100 (Calories from Fat 45); Total Fat 5g (Saturated Fat 0g; Trans Fat 0g); Cholesterol 105mg; Sodium 270mg; Total Carbohydrate 0g (Dietary Fiber 0g; Sugars 0g); Protein 12g **% Daily Value:** Vitamin A 6%; Vitamin C 6%; Calcium 4%; Iron 10% **Exchanges:** 1 1/2 Very Lean Meat, 1 Fat **Carbohydrate Choices:** 0

Lemon and Herb Salmon Packets

Prep Time: 20 minutes | **Start to Finish:** 40 minutes | 2 servings

1 1/4 cups reduced-sodium chicken broth

1 cup uncooked instant brown rice

1/2 cup matchstick-cut carrots (from 10-oz bag)

1/2 to 3/4 lb salmon fillets, cut into 2 serving pieces

1/2 teaspoon lemon-pepper seasoning

2 tablespoons chopped fresh chives

2 lemon slices (1/4 inch thick)

1 Heat gas or charcoal grill. In 1-quart saucepan, heat broth to boiling over high heat. Stir in rice. Reduce heat to low; cover and simmer 5 minutes or until most of broth is absorbed. Stir in carrots.

2 Meanwhile, cut 2 (18 × 12-inch) sheets of heavy-duty foil; spray with cooking spray. Place fish fillet on center of each sheet. Sprinkle with lemon-pepper seasoning; top with chives. Arrange lemon slices over fish.

3 Spoon rice mixture around each fish fillet. Bring up 2 sides of foil over fish so edges meet. Seal edges, making tight 1/2-inch fold; fold again, allowing space for heat circulation and expansion. Fold other sides to seal.

4 Place packets on grill. Cover grill; cook over low heat 16 to 20 minutes or until fish flakes easily with fork. To serve, cut large X across top of each packet; carefully fold back foil to allow steam to escape.

BAKING DIRECTIONS: Heat oven to 450°F. Make packets as directed. Place packets in 15 × 10-inch pan with sides. Bake 16 to 20 minutes or until fish flakes easily with fork.

tip for *two*

Salmon contains a fat that has heart-protective benefits, omega-3 fatty acids. Baking your dinner in foil means minimal cleanup.

1 Serving: Calories 380 (Calories from Fat 70); Total Fat 8g (Saturated Fat 2g; Trans Fat 0g); Cholesterol 75mg; Sodium 540mg; Total Carbohydrate 47g (Dietary Fiber 3g; Sugars 2g); Protein 31g   **% Daily Value:** Vitamin A 80%; Vitamin C 8%; Calcium 4%; Iron 10%   **Exchanges:** 3 Starch, 3 Very Lean Meat, 1 Fat   **Carbohydrate Choices:** 3

Grilled Bourbon-Mustard Tuna

Prep Time: 30 minutes | **Start to Finish:** 1 hour 30 minutes | 2 servings

3/4 lb tuna steaks (1 inch thick), cut into 2 serving pieces

1/4 cup packed brown sugar

1/2 teaspoon salt

2 tablespoons bourbon or apple juice

2 teaspoons Dijon mustard

2 medium green onions, sliced (2 tablespoons)

1 In 8-inch square (2-quart) glass baking dish, place fish. In small bowl, mix brown sugar, salt, bourbon, mustard and onions; pour over fish. Cover; refrigerate 1 hour to marinate.

2 Heat gas or charcoal grill. Remove fish from marinade; pour marinade into 1-quart saucepan and reserve. Carefully brush grill rack with canola oil. Place fish on grill. Cover grill; cook over medium heat 10 to 15 minutes, turning once, until fish flakes easily with fork and is slightly pink in center.

3 Heat marinade to boiling; pour over fish.

BROILING DIRECTIONS: Marinate fish as directed. Set oven control to broil. Brush broiler pan rack with canola oil (do not spray). Place fish on rack in pan. Broil with tops about 4 inches from heat 10 to 15 minutes, turning once, until fish flakes easily with fork and is slightly pink in center.

tip for *two*

Fresh tuna is done when it's still partially pink in the center. If you grill it longer, it may become overdone, so watch it carefully.

1 Serving: Calories 330 (Calories from Fat 80); Total Fat 9g (Saturated Fat 2.5g; Trans Fat 0g); Cholesterol 100mg; Sodium 820mg; Total Carbohydrate 28g (Dietary Fiber 0g; Sugars 27g); Protein 33g **% Daily Value:** Vitamin A 6%; Vitamin C 4%; Calcium 4%; Iron 10% **Exchanges:** 2 Other Carbohydrate, 4 1/2 Very Lean Meat, 1 1/2 Fat **Carbohydrate Choices:** 2

Sole Provençale

Prep Time: 25 minutes | **Start to Finish:** 30 minutes | 2 servings

1/2 cup sliced fresh mushrooms (about 1 oz)

2 tablespoons dry white wine or nonalcoholic white wine

2 teaspoons tomato paste

1 medium tomato, chopped (3/4 cup)

1 small onion, chopped (1/4 cup)

1 clove garlic, finely chopped

2 teaspoons chopped fresh thyme

1/4 teaspoon salt

1/2 lb thin sole fillets, cut into 2 serving pieces

2 teaspoons canola oil

1 In 1-quart saucepan, heat mushrooms, wine, tomato paste, tomato, onion, garlic and half of the thyme to boiling; reduce heat to medium. Cook about 5 minutes, stirring occasionally, until slightly thickened.

2 Meanwhile, sprinkle salt and remaining thyme over fish fillets; roll up fillets. In 8-inch nonstick skillet, heat oil over medium-high heat. Cook rolled fish, seam side down, in oil 4 to 5 minutes, turning as needed, until lightly browned on all sides.

3 Top fish with tomato mixture; reduce heat to low. Cover; cook 5 minutes longer or until fish flakes easily with fork.

tip for *two*

Cooking foods, especially fish, with wine adds an extra boost of flavor. You'll notice several recipes in this chapter use wine as an ingredient. A substitute, like apple juice, is usually given, or you might try nonalcoholic wine.

1 Serving: Calories 170 (Calories from Fat 50); Total Fat 6g (Saturated Fat 0.5g; Trans Fat 0g); Cholesterol 55mg; Sodium 430mg; Total Carbohydrate 7g (Dietary Fiber 2g; Sugars 4g); Protein 21g   **% Daily Value:** Vitamin A 15%; Vitamin C 10%; Calcium 4%; Iron 6%   **Exchanges:** 1 Vegetable, 2 1/2 Very Lean Meat, 1 Fat   **Carbohydrate Choices:** 1/2

Greek Cod

Prep Time: 20 minutes | Start to Finish: 40 minutes | 2 servings

1 tablespoon olive oil

1 small onion, finely chopped (1/4 cup)

1 clove garlic, finely chopped

1 teaspoon grated lemon peel

1 tablespoon chopped fresh or 1 teaspoon dried basil leaves

1 teaspoon chopped fresh or 1/4 teaspoon dried thyme leaves

1 can (14.5 oz) diced tomatoes, undrained

3/4 lb cod or other mild flavor, medium-firm fish fillets, cut into 2 serving pieces

2 tablespoons chopped ripe olives

2 tablespoons crumbled reduced-fat feta cheese

2 tablespoons plain croutons

1 Heat oven to 400°F. In 10-inch skillet, heat oil over medium-high heat. Cook onion and garlic in oil 2 to 3 minutes, stirring frequently, until onion is soft.

2 Stir in lemon peel, basil, thyme and tomatoes. Cook over medium-high heat about 6 minutes, stirring occasionally, until mixture is slightly thickened.

3 Spoon half of tomato mixture into 8-inch square (2-quart) glass baking dish. Top with fish. Spoon remaining tomato mixture over fish. Sprinkle with olives, cheese and croutons.

4 Bake uncovered 15 to 20 minutes or until fish flakes easily with fork.

tip for two

The herbs, lemon, olives and feta cheese are a great combination for fresh cod. Serve with long-grain rice or whole wheat couscous and a green or orange vegetable.

1 Serving: Calories 300 (Calories from Fat 100); Total Fat 11g (Saturated Fat 2.5g; Trans Fat 0g); Cholesterol 95mg; Sodium 610mg; Total Carbohydrate 13g (Dietary Fiber 3g; Sugars 6g); Protein 36g   % Daily Value: Vitamin A 10%; Vitamin C 20%; Calcium 15%; Iron 15%   Exchanges: 1/2 Other Carbohydrate, 1 Vegetable, 5 Very Lean Meat, 1 1/2 Fat Carbohydrate Choices: 1

Dilled Halibut Steaks

Prep Time: 5 minutes | **Start to Finish:** 30 minutes | 2 servings

3/4 lb halibut steaks (1 inch thick), cut into 2 serving pieces

1/8 teaspoon salt

2 sprigs dill weed

2 lemon slices (1/4 inch thick)

2 tablespoons dry white wine or nonalcoholic white wine

1 Heat oven to 400°F. Spray 8-inch square (2-quart) glass baking dish with cooking spray. Pat fish dry with paper towels; place in baking dish.

2 Sprinkle fish with salt. Place dill weed sprig and lemon slice on each fish piece. Pour wine over fish.

3 Bake uncovered 20 to 25 minutes or until fish flakes easily with fork.

tip for *two*

Fresh dill nicely complements the halibut, but other fresh herbs, like tarragon or basil, would be good choices, too.

1 Serving: Calories 150 (Calories from Fat 20); Total Fat 2g (Saturated Fat 0g; Trans Fat 0g); Cholesterol 90mg; Sodium 290mg; Total Carbohydrate 0g (Dietary Fiber 0g; Sugars 0g); Protein 32g **% Daily Value:** Vitamin A 0%; Vitamin C 4%; Calcium 2%; Iron 2% **Exchanges:** 4 1/2 Very Lean Meat **Carbohydrate Choices:** 0

Walnut-Coated Walleye

Prep Time: 20 minutes | **Start to Finish:** 20 minutes | 2 servings

3/4 lb walleye fillets, cut into 2 serving pieces

2 tablespoons all-purpose flour

1 egg or 2 egg whites

1 tablespoon water

1/4 cup all-purpose flour

1/4 cup finely chopped walnuts

1 tablespoon chopped fresh chives

1/4 teaspoon salt

1/8 teaspoon pepper

2 teaspoons canola oil

1 Rinse fish; pat dry with paper towels. Place 2 tablespoons flour on sheet of waxed paper. In shallow dish, beat egg and water with fork or wire whisk until well mixed. In another shallow dish, mix 1/4 cup flour, the walnuts, chives, salt and pepper.

2 Coat fish with flour, then dip into egg mixture. Coat both sides with walnut mixture.

3 In 10-inch nonstick skillet, heat oil over medium heat. Cook fish in oil 5 to 10 minutes, turning once, until fish flakes easily with fork.

tip for *two*

Coating the fish with walnuts adds flavor and crunch. Because walnuts are high in fat (a good fat for your heart), they can become rancid, so it's a good idea to taste before using them if you've had them for a while.

1 Serving: Calories 420 (Calories from Fat 170); Total Fat 19g (Saturated Fat 2.5g; Trans Fat 0g); Cholesterol 200mg; Sodium 470mg; Total Carbohydrate 20g (Dietary Fiber 2g; Sugars 0g); Protein 41g   **% Daily Value:** Vitamin A 6%; Vitamin C 0%; Calcium 6%; Iron 15%   **Exchanges:** 1 1/2 Starch, 5 Very Lean Meat, 3 Fat   **Carbohydrate Choices:** 1

Orange-Ginger Beef Kabobs

Prep Time: 20 minutes | **Start to Finish:** 8 hours 20 minutes | 2 servings

1/4 cup orange marmalade

1 tablespoon white wine vinegar

1/4 teaspoon ground ginger

1 clove garlic, finely chopped

1/2 lb boneless beef sirloin steak (about 1 inch thick), fat removed, cut into 1-inch cubes

1 In small glass or plastic bowl, mix all ingredients except beef. Stir in beef. Cover; refrigerate at least 2 hours to marinate but no longer than 8 hours, stirring occasionally.

2 Set oven control to broil. Remove beef from marinade; reserve marinade. On each of 2 (11-inch) metal skewers, thread beef cubes, leaving 1/4 inch space between each cube. Place on rack in broiler pan.

3 Broil with tops about 5 inches from heat 4 minutes. Turn; brush with reserved marinade. Broil 3 to 5 minutes longer or until brown and medium doneness.

GRILLING DIRECTIONS: Heat gas or charcoal grill. Make kabobs as directed. Place on grill. Cover grill; cook over medium heat 7 to 9 minutes, turning and brushing 2 or 3 times with reserved marinade, until brown and medium doneness.

tip for *two*

Marinating makes for great flavor and tenderness, but it takes a little time and planning. If you marinate the beef before you leave in the morning, the kabobs will be ready to cook when you return home, a good use of time.

1 Serving: Calories 250 (Calories from Fat 35); Total Fat 3.5g (Saturated Fat 1g; Trans Fat 0g); Cholesterol 65mg; Sodium 45mg; Total Carbohydrate 29g (Dietary Fiber 0g; Sugars 20g); Protein 26g **% Daily Value:** Vitamin A 0%; Vitamin C 4%; Calcium 0%; Iron 15% **Exchanges:** 2 Other Carbohydrate, 3 1/2 Very Lean Meat, 1/2 Fat **Carbohydrate Choices:** 2

5 *easy* Coatings for Fish and Seafood

Pick a super-easy coating for fish fillets or seafood. Bake or cook in a skillet with a little bit of canola oil.

1 Chili-Cornmeal

Dip in chili sauce or taco seasoning, then coat with cornmeal.

2 Parmesan-Creole

Dip in reduced-fat or fat-free mayonnaise, then coat with grated Parmesan cheese mixed with Creole or Cajun seasoning or chili powder.

3 Honey-Nut

Dip in honey or honey mustard, then coat with finely chopped almonds, walnuts or peanuts.

4 Mustard-Pretzel

Dip in yellow or Dijon mustard, then coat with crushed pretzels.

5 Lemon-Herb

Coat with grated lemon peel, finely chopped bread crumbs and finely chopped parsley, rosemary or basil.

Grilled Greek-Style Steak

Prep Time: 15 minutes | **Start to Finish:** 15 minutes | 2 servings

1/2 lb boneless beef top sirloin, cut into 2 pieces

1 teaspoon finely chopped garlic

1/4 teaspoon lemon-pepper seasoning

1/4 cup lightly packed chopped fresh spinach leaves

1/4 cup crumbled reduced-fat feta cheese (1 oz)

1 tablespoon chopped ripe olives

1 Heat gas or charcoal grill. Rub both sides of each piece of beef with garlic; sprinkle with lemon-pepper seasoning.

2 Place beef on grill. Cover grill; cook over medium heat 9 to 11 minutes, turning once, until beef is desired doneness.

3 In small bowl, mix remaining ingredients. Spoon over beef.

tip for *two*

For a more authentic Greek topping, use pitted and chopped kalamata olives in place of the ripe olives and serve with sliced fresh tomatoes.

1 Serving: Calories 180 (Calories from Fat 60); Total Fat 6g (Saturated Fat 3g; Trans Fat 0g); Cholesterol 70mg; Sodium 350mg; Total Carbohydrate 2g (Dietary Fiber 0g; Sugars 0g); Protein 30g **% Daily Value:** Vitamin A 10%; Vitamin C 0%; Calcium 6%; Iron 15% **Exchanges:** 4 1/2 Very Lean Meat, 1/2 Fat **Carbohydrate Choices:** 0

Italian Minute Steaks

Prep Time: 10 minutes | **Start to Finish:** 30 minutes | 2 servings

2 beef cube steaks (4 oz each)

1/4 teaspoon lemon-pepper
seasoning

2 teaspoons canola oil

1 cup tomato pasta sauce

1 small onion, thinly sliced,
separated into rings

1/2 small green bell pepper,
chopped (1/4 cup)

2 tablespoons grated Parmesan
cheese

1 Sprinkle beef steaks with lemon-pepper seasoning. In 10-inch nonstick skillet, heat oil over medium heat. Cook steaks in oil about 10 minutes, turning once, until brown.

2 Spoon half of the pasta sauce over steaks. Layer onion and bell pepper on top; spoon remaining sauce over vegetables. Sprinkle with cheese; reduce heat to low.

3 Cover; simmer about 10 minutes or until sauce is hot and vegetables are crisp-tender.

tip for *two*

These minute steaks are just that—ready in minutes. They're so fast, it's hard to think of something to serve with them. A pasta side dish like couscous, also quick-cooking, is perfect.

1 Serving: Calories 400 (Calories from Fat 170); Total Fat 18g (Saturated Fat 5g; Trans Fat 0g); Cholesterol 55mg; Sodium 810mg; Total Carbohydrate 28g (Dietary Fiber 3g; Sugars 14g); Protein 31g   **% Daily Value:** Vitamin A 15%; Vitamin C 25%; Calcium 15%; Iron 20%   **Exchanges:** 1 1/2 Other Carbohydrate, 1 Vegetable, 4 Lean Meat, 1 1/2 Fat **Carbohydrate Choices:** 2

Mini Meat Loaves

Prep Time: 10 minutes | **Start to Finish:** 40 minutes | 2 servings

1 tablespoon fat-free (skim) milk

1 egg white

2 teaspoons Worcestershire sauce

1/2 lb extra-lean (at least 90%) ground beef

2 tablespoons dry bread crumbs (any flavor)

1/4 teaspoon salt

1/4 teaspoon pepper

1 tablespoon barbecue sauce

Strips of cheese, if desired

1 Heat oven to 350°F. In medium bowl, beat milk, egg and Worcestershire sauce with fork. Mix in beef, bread crumbs, salt and pepper. Shape into 2 (4 × 2 1/2-inch) loaves. Place in ungreased 8-inch square pan. Brush loaves with barbecue sauce.

2 Bake 18 to 22 minutes until meat thermometer inserted in center of loaf reads 160°F.

3 Decorate loaves with strips of cheese. Let stand 5 minutes.

tip for *two*

These mini loaves bake in half the time of regular meat loaves. The secret? Their size, perfect for two. Serve with mashed or baked potatoes.

1 Serving: Calories 220 (Calories from Fat 90); Total Fat 9g (Saturated Fat 4g; Trans Fat 0.5g); Cholesterol 70mg; Sodium 560mg; Total Carbohydrate 9g (Dietary Fiber 0g; Sugars 4g); Protein 25g   **% Daily Value:** Vitamin A 0%; Vitamin C 0%; Calcium 4%; Iron 20%   **Exchanges:** 1/2 Other Carbohydrate, 3 1/2 Lean Meat   **Carbohydrate Choices:** 1/2

Grilled Bourbon-Glazed Beef Kabobs

Prep Time: 25 minutes | **Start to Finish:** 25 minutes | 2 servings

GLAZE

2 tablespoons bourbon or water

1 tablespoon teriyaki baste and glaze (from 12-oz bottle)

1 tablespoon frozen (thawed) orange juice concentrate

1/4 cup packed brown sugar

Dash crushed red pepper flakes

KABOBS

1/2 lb beef top sirloin, cut into 1 1/2-inch cubes

8 pieces (1 1/2-inch) red onion

8 fresh whole mushrooms

8 pieces (1 1/2-inch) red bell pepper

1 teaspoon olive oil

1/4 teaspoon salt

1 Heat gas or charcoal grill. In 1-quart saucepan, mix 1 tablespoon of the bourbon, the teriyaki glaze, orange juice concentrate, brown sugar and crushed red pepper. Heat to boiling over medium heat; reduce heat to low. Simmer 5 minutes, stirring occasionally; remove from heat. Stir in remaining 1 tablespoon bourbon. Reserve 2 tablespoons glaze.

2 In medium bowl, place beef, onion, mushrooms and bell pepper. Drizzle with oil; toss to coat. Sprinkle with salt; toss to coat. On each of 2 (10- to 12-inch) metal skewers, thread beef, onion, mushrooms and bell pepper alternately, leaving 1/4-inch space between each piece.

3 Place kabobs on grill. Cover grill; cook over medium heat 9 to 11 minutes, turning once and brushing with glaze during last 3 minutes, until beef is desired doneness and vegetables are tender.

4 Just before serving, generously brush kabobs with reserved 2 tablespoons glaze.

tip for *two*

Add more color to these kabobs by using a variety of colored bell peppers, including red, green, yellow or orange. Serve over cooked brown rice or quick-cooking barley.

1 Serving: Calories 370 (Calories from Fat 60); Total Fat 6g (Saturated Fat 1.5g; Trans Fat 0g); Cholesterol 65mg; Sodium 550mg; Total Carbohydrate 46g (Dietary Fiber 4g; Sugars 39g); Protein 30g **% Daily Value:** Vitamin A 40%; Vitamin C 110%; Calcium 6%; Iron 20% **Exchanges:** 2 1/2 Other Carbohydrate, 1 Vegetable, 4 Very Lean Meat, 1 Fat **Carbohydrate Choices:** 3

Southwest Herb Flank Steak

Prep Time: 10 minutes | Start to Finish: 40 minutes | 2 servings

1/2 lb beef flank steak

1/2 cup chopped plum (Roma) tomatoes (2 or 3 medium)

2 tablespoons lime juice

2 tablespoons chopped fresh cilantro

2 teaspoons chopped fresh oregano

1/8 teaspoon salt

1 Make cuts about 1/2 inch apart and 1/4 inch deep in diamond pattern in both sides of beef; place in large resealable food-storage plastic bag or ungreased 8-inch square glass baking dish.

2 In small bowl, mix remaining ingredients; spoon over beef. Seal bag or cover dish with plastic wrap. Let stand at room temperature 15 minutes.

3 Set oven control to broil. Spray broiler pan rack with cooking spray. Place beef on rack in broiler pan; brush with liquid from bag or dish. Reserve tomatoes. Broil with top of beef 4 to 6 inches from heat 8 to 12 minutes or until desired doneness, turning once.

4 With slotted spoon, spoon tomatoes onto beef; discard remaining liquid. Broil 3 to 5 minutes longer until tomatoes are lightly browned. Cut beef diagonally across grain into thin slices to serve.

tip for *two*

Serve this excellent steak with fresh green beans and red bell pepper strips sautéed in olive oil.

1 Serving: Calories 190 (Calories from Fat 70); Total Fat 8g (Saturated Fat 3g; Trans Fat 0g); Cholesterol 50mg; Sodium 190mg; Total Carbohydrate 3g (Dietary Fiber 0g; Sugars 2g); Protein 27g   **% Daily Value:** Vitamin A 10%; Vitamin C 8%; Calcium 2%; Iron 15%   **Exchanges:** 4 Very Lean Meat, 1 Fat   **Carbohydrate Choices:** 0

Sherried Pork with Pine Nuts

Prep Time: 25 minutes | **Start to Finish:** 45 minutes | 2 servings

1/2 lb boneless pork loin or leg, cut into thin bite-size pieces

1 teaspoon cornstarch

1 tablespoon reduced-sodium soy sauce

Dash white pepper

1 teaspoon cornstarch

2 tablespoons sherry, dry white wine or water

1 tablespoon canola oil

1 clove garlic, finely chopped

1 medium onion, thinly sliced (1/2 cup)

1/2 medium red bell pepper, thinly sliced (1/2 cup)

1 medium stalk celery, diagonally sliced (1/2 cup)

2 tablespoons reduced-sodium chicken broth

2 tablespoons pine nuts, toasted (page 70)

1 In small glass or plastic bowl, toss pork, 1 teaspoon cornstarch, the soy sauce and white pepper. Cover; refrigerate 20 minutes to marinate.

2 In small bowl, mix 1 teaspoon cornstarch and the sherry; set aside.

3 Heat 12-inch skillet over high heat until 1 or 2 drops of water bubble and skitter when sprinkled in skillet. Add oil; rotate skillet to coat. Add pork and garlic; cook about 3 minutes, stirring frequently, until pork is no longer pink.

4 Stir in onion, bell pepper and celery. Cook 2 minutes, stirring frequently. Stir in broth; heat to boiling. Stir in cornstarch mixture. Cook and stir about 10 seconds or until thickened. Stir in nuts.

tip for *two*

To make Sherried Chicken with Pine Nuts, substitute 2 boneless skinless chicken breasts for the pork. Cut chicken into 1/8-inch strips.

1 Serving: Calories 350 (Calories from Fat 190); Total Fat 21g (Saturated Fat 4.5g; Trans Fat 0g); Cholesterol 70mg; Sodium 370mg; Total Carbohydrate 11g (Dietary Fiber 2g; Sugars 3g); Protein 28g **% Daily Value:** Vitamin A 15%; Vitamin C 40%; Calcium 2%; Iron 8% **Exchanges:** 1/2 Starch, 4 Lean Meat, 2 Fat **Carbohydrate Choices:** 1

Chili-Ranch Grilled Pork

Prep Time: 25 minutes | **Start to Finish:** 40 minutes | 2 servings

2 boneless pork loin chops, 3/4 inch thick (4 oz each)

2 tablespoons reduced-fat ranch dressing

1/4 teaspoon salt

1/4 teaspoon chili powder

1/8 teaspoon dried thyme leaves

1/8 teaspoon garlic powder

1 Heat gas or charcoal grill. Place pork chops in shallow bowl. Pour dressing over both sides of pork chops. Cover; refrigerate 15 minutes.

2 Meanwhile, in small bowl, mix remaining ingredients. Remove pork from marinade; discard marinade.

3 Sprinkle half of seasoning mixture over one side of pork chops. Place pork on grill, seasoned side down. Sprinkle remaining seasoning mixture over pork. Cover grill; cook over medium heat 8 to 10 minutes, turning once, or until no longer pink and meat thermometer inserted in center reads 160°F.

tip for *two*

Try this recipe using boneless skinless chicken breasts. Grill 15 to 20 minutes or until the juice of the chicken is clear when center of thickest part is cut (170°F).

1 Serving: Calories 210 (Calories from Fat 100); Total Fat 11g (Saturated Fat 3g; Trans Fat 0g); Cholesterol 75mg; Sodium 480mg; Total Carbohydrate 3g (Dietary Fiber 0g; Sugars 0g); Protein 24g **% Daily Value:** Vitamin A 2%; Vitamin C 0%; Calcium 2%; Iron 6% **Exchanges:** 3 1/2 Very Lean Meat, 2 Fat **Carbohydrate Choices:** 0

Grilled Pork and Sweet Potato Kabobs

Prep Time: 15 minutes | **Start to Finish:** 20 minutes | 2 servings (2 kabobs each)

1/3 cup orange marmalade

1 teaspoon finely chopped fresh rosemary leaves

1/4 teaspoon salt

1/2 lb dark-orange sweet potatoes, peeled, cut into 8 pieces

2 tablespoons water

1/2 lb pork tenderloin, cut into 1-inch pieces

1 small zucchini, cut into 8 slices

1 Heat gas or charcoal grill. In 1-quart saucepan, heat marmalade, rosemary and salt to boiling, stirring frequently. Remove from heat; set aside.

2 In 1-quart microwavable bowl, place sweet potato pieces and water. Cover loosely with microwavable paper towel. Microwave on High 2 to 3 minutes, stirring once, just until potatoes are tender (do not overcook). Drain sweet potatoes; rinse with cold water.

3 On each of 4 (10- to 12-inch) metal skewers, carefully thread pork, sweet potatoes and zucchini (with cut side facing out) alternately, leaving 1/4-inch space between each piece.

4 Place kabobs on grill. Cover grill; cook over medium heat 8 to 10 minutes, turning once and brushing with marmalade glaze during last 3 minutes, until pork is no longer pink in center.

tip for *two*

For the best flavor and most nutrients, purchase dark-orange sweet potatoes, sometimes called yams, at the grocery store.

1 Serving: Calories 410 (Calories from Fat 40); Total Fat 4.5g (Saturated Fat 1.5g; Trans Fat 0g); Cholesterol 70mg; Sodium 410mg; Total Carbohydrate 62g (Dietary Fiber 5g; Sugars 37g); Protein 29g **% Daily Value:** Vitamin A 440%; Vitamin C 30%; Calcium 6%; Iron 15% **Exchanges:** 1 1/2 Starch, 2 1/2 Other Carbohydrate, 3 1/2 Very Lean Meat, 1/2 Fat **Carbohydrate Choices:** 4

Spicy Pork Chops

Prep Time: 5 minutes | **Start to Finish:** 45 minutes | 2 servings

1 teaspoon chili powder

1 teaspoon canola oil

1/2 teaspoon ground cumin

Dash ground red pepper (cayenne)

1/8 teaspoon salt

1 large clove garlic, finely chopped

2 pork loin or rib chops, about 1/2 inch thick (about 5 oz each)

1 In small bowl, mix all ingredients except pork. Cut outer edge of fat on pork chops diagonally at 1-inch intervals to prevent curling (do not cut into meat). Spread chili powder mixture evenly on both sides of pork. Cover; refrigerate at least 30 minutes to marinate.

2 Heat closed medium-size contact grill for 5 to 10 minutes. Place pork on grill. Close grill. Grill 8 to 10 minutes or until no longer pink when cut near bone.

tip for *two*

Look for individually packed pork chops in the freezer section of your grocery store. They're a handy way to buy pork chops because you can get only as many as you need.

1 Serving: Calories 190 (Calories from Fat 90); Total Fat 10g (Saturated Fat 3g; Trans Fat 0g); Cholesterol 65mg; Sodium 200mg; Total Carbohydrate 1g (Dietary Fiber 0g; Sugars 0g); Protein 22g **% Daily Value:** Vitamin A 8%; Vitamin C 0%; Calcium 0%; Iron 8% **Exchanges:** 3 Lean Meat, 1/2 Fat **Carbohydrate Choices:** 0

Grilled Pork Tenderloin with Pineapple Salsa

Prep Time: 25 minutes | **Start to Finish:** 25 minutes | 2 servings

1/2 teaspoon finely chopped gingerroot or 1/4 teaspoon ground ginger

1/2 teaspoon salt

1/4 teaspoon ground cumin

1/2 lb pork tenderloin

1 kiwifruit, peeled, chopped

1 slice (1/2-inch-thick) pineapple, rind removed, cut into 1/2-inch pieces

1 tablespoon orange marmalade

1 teaspoon finely chopped jalapeño chile

1 Heat gas or charcoal grill. In small bowl, mix gingerroot, salt and cumin. Rub pork with gingerroot mixture.

2 Place pork on grill. Cover grill; cook over medium heat 15 to 20 minutes, turning occasionally, until pork has slight blush of pink in center and meat thermometer inserted in center reads 160°F.

3 Meanwhile, in small bowl, stir remaining ingredients until marmalade is completely mixed in.

4 Cut pork into thin slices. Serve with pineapple salsa.

tip for two

You may have to ask the butcher to cut a 1/2-pound piece of a larger tenderloin for this recipe. Serve with papaya slices to enhance the flavors of the pineapple salsa.

1 Serving: Calories 220 (Calories from Fat 40); Total Fat 4.5g (Saturated Fat 1.5g; Trans Fat 0g); Cholesterol 70mg; Sodium 650mg; Total Carbohydrate 18g (Dietary Fiber 2g; Sugars 12g); Protein 26g **% Daily Value:** Vitamin A 0%; Vitamin C 45%; Calcium 2%; Iron 10% **Exchanges:** 1/2 Fruit, 1/2 Other Carbohydrate, 3 1/2 Very Lean Meat, 1 Fat **Carbohydrate Choices:** 1

Grilled Spicy Chipotle Barbecue Turkey Drumsticks

Prep Time: 35 minutes | Start to Finish: 35 minutes | 2 servings

1 tablespoon finely chopped onion

2 teaspoons water

1/4 cup barbecue sauce

2 tablespoons apricot preserves

1 teaspoon chopped chipotle chile in adobo sauce (from 7-oz can)

1/8 teaspoon salt

2 turkey drumsticks (8 oz each)

1 Heat gas or charcoal grill. In 1-quart saucepan, cook onion and water over medium heat 3 to 5 minutes, stirring occasionally, until onion is tender. Stir in barbecue sauce, preserves, chile and salt. Cook 1 to 2 minutes, stirring occasionally, until heated through. Reserve 3 tablespoons sauce.

2 Place drumsticks on grill. Cover grill; cook over medium-low heat 25 to 30 minutes, turning frequently and brushing with sauce during last 5 minutes, until juice of turkey is clear when thickest part is cut to bone (180°F).

3 Serve drumsticks with reserved 3 tablespoons sauce.

tip for two

Turkey drumsticks come in various weights. Try to purchase two at close to the same weight. If the drumsticks are heavier, you will need to grill them longer.

1 Serving: Calories 350 (Calories from Fat 110); Total Fat 12g (Saturated Fat 4g; Trans Fat 0g); Cholesterol 95mg; Sodium 560mg; Total Carbohydrate 26g (Dietary Fiber 0g; Sugars 18g); Protein 33g % Daily Value: Vitamin A 4%; Vitamin C 2%; Calcium 6%; Iron 15% Exchanges: 1 1/2 Other Carbohydrate, 4 1/2 Lean Meat Carbohydrate Choices: 2

Savory Chicken Stew and Dumplings

Prep Time: 15 minutes | **Start to Finish:** 35 minutes | 2 servings

3 tablespoons all-purpose flour

1/4 teaspoon dried sage leaves

1/4 teaspoon dried thyme leaves

1/8 teaspoon pepper

1 cup reduced-sodium chicken broth

1 1/2 cups frozen mixed vegetables (from 1-lb bag)

1 cup cut-up cooked chicken breast

1/2 cup Original Bisquick® mix

1 tablespoon chopped green onion

Dash onion powder

3 tablespoons fat-free (skim) milk

1 In 1 1/2-quart nonstick saucepan, mix flour, sage, thyme and pepper. Gradually stir in broth with wire whisk until blended. Heat to boiling over medium heat, stirring constantly. Stir in mixed vegetables and chicken; heat to boiling.

2 In small bowl, mix Bisquick mix, onion and onion powder. Stir in milk just until moistened. Drop dough by 6 spoonfuls onto boiling stew; reduce heat to low.

3 Simmer uncovered 10 minutes. Cover; simmer 10 minutes longer.

tip for two

This stew for two is perfect for a cozy evening. You can vary the flavors by using different herbs, like rosemary or parsley, different frozen veggies and turkey instead of chicken.

1 Serving: Calories 380 (Calories from Fat 70); Total Fat 8g (Saturated Fat 2g; Trans Fat 0.5g); Cholesterol 60mg; Sodium 810mg; Total Carbohydrate 47g (Dietary Fiber 7g; Sugars 8g); Protein 31g **% Daily Value:** Vitamin A 120%; Vitamin C 4%; Calcium 15%; Iron 20% **Exchanges:** 2 Starch, 1 Other Carbohydrate, 1 Vegetable, 3 Very Lean Meat, 1 Fat **Carbohydrate Choices:** 3

Chicken and Penne Primavera

Prep Time: 25 minutes | **Start to Finish:** 25 minutes | 2 servings

1 cup uncooked penne or mostaccioli pasta (3 1/2 oz)

1 teaspoon olive oil

1/2 lb boneless skinless chicken breasts, cut into 1-inch pieces

1/2 cup sliced zucchini

1/2 cup sliced yellow summer squash

1/2 cup 2-inch pieces asparagus

1/4 cup reduced-fat Italian dressing

2 tablespoons chopped fresh basil leaves

3 tablespoons shredded Parmesan cheese

Coarsely ground pepper, if desired

1 Cook and drain pasta as directed on package, omitting salt.

2 Meanwhile, in 12-inch skillet, heat oil over medium-high heat. Cook chicken in oil about 5 minutes, stirring occasionally, until brown on outside and no longer pink in center.

3 Stir in zucchini, squash and asparagus. Cook about 5 minutes, stirring occasionally, until vegetables are crisp-tender.

4 Stir pasta into chicken mixture. Stir in dressing and basil; cook until thoroughly heated. Sprinkle with cheese and pepper.

tip for *two*

Primavera is a combination of vegetables. You can slice all the vegetables ahead of time and refrigerate up to 3 hours before using.

1 Serving: Calories 520 (Calories from Fat 140); Total Fat 15g (Saturated Fat 4g; Trans Fat 0g); Cholesterol 75mg; Sodium 620mg; Total Carbohydrate 55g (Dietary Fiber 5g; Sugars 4g); Protein 39g **% Daily Value:** Vitamin A 10%; Vitamin C 15%; Calcium 15%; Iron 20% **Exchanges:** 3 Starch, 1 1/2 Vegetable, 4 Very Lean Meat, 2 Fat **Carbohydrate Choices:** 3 1/2

Grilled Chicken Citrus Teriyaki

Prep Time: 25 minutes | **Start to Finish:** 55 minutes | 2 servings

1/4 cup teriyaki baste and glaze (from 12-oz bottle)

1/4 cup frozen (thawed) orange juice concentrate

2 teaspoons grated orange peel

1/2 lb uncooked chicken breast tenders (not breaded)

1 cup sugar snap pea pods

1 cup sliced fresh mushrooms (3 oz)

1 medium zucchini, cut into 1/2-inch slices (2 cups)

1/2 medium red bell pepper, cut into 1-inch pieces (3/4 cup)

1 In small bowl, mix teriyaki glaze, orange juice concentrate and orange peel. Reserve 2 tablespoons mixture. Add chicken to remaining mixture; toss to coat. Cover; refrigerate 30 minutes to marinate.

2 Meanwhile, heat gas or charcoal grill. Place grill basket (grill "wok") on grill over medium heat. Remove chicken from marinade; discard marinade. Place chicken in grill basket.

3 Place basket on grill. Cover grill; cook over medium heat 6 to 8 minutes, shaking basket or stirring chicken occasionally, until chicken is brown.

4 Add remaining ingredients to grill basket. Place basket on grill. Cover grill; cook 6 to 8 minutes, shaking basket or stirring occasionally, until vegetables are crisp-tender and chicken is no longer pink in center. Add 2 tablespoons reserved marinade; stir to coat vegetables and chicken. Cover grill; cook 2 to 3 minutes longer or until thoroughly heated.

tip for *two*

For a different citrus flavor, try using grated lime or lemon peel instead of orange.

1 Serving: Calories 270 (Calories from Fat 10); Total Fat 1g (Saturated Fat 0g; Trans Fat 0g); Cholesterol 50mg; Sodium 960mg; Total Carbohydrate 34g (Dietary Fiber 4g; Sugars 28g); Protein 30g **% Daily Value:** Vitamin A 35%; Vitamin C 130%; Calcium 8%; Iron 15% **Exchanges:** 1 1/2 Other Carbohydrate, 2 Vegetable, 3 1/2 Very Lean Meat **Carbohydrate Choices:** 2

Grilled Chicken Breasts Italian

Prep Time: 1 hour 15 minutes | **Start to Finish:** 55 minutes | 2 servings

2 bone-in skin-on chicken breast halves (about 1 1/4 lb)

1/4 cup dry red wine or nonalcoholic red wine

1 tablespoon olive oil

1 teaspoon Italian seasoning

1 clove garlic, finely chopped

1 Place chicken in shallow glass dish or plastic bag. In small bowl, mix remaining ingredients; pour over chicken. Cover; refrigerate at least 1 hour to marinate but no longer than 6 hours.

2 Heat gas or charcoal grill. Remove chicken from marinade; reserve marinade. Place chicken, bone sides down, on grill. Cover grill; cook over medium heat 10 to 20 minutes. Turn chicken; cover grill. Cook 15 to 20 minutes longer, turning and brushing 2 or 3 times with marinade, until juice of chicken is clear when thickest part is cut to bone (170°F).

BROILING DIRECTIONS: Marinate chicken as directed. Set oven control to broil. Place chicken, skin sides down, on rack in broiler pan. Broil with tops about 4 inches from heat 10 to 20 minutes. Turn chicken; brush with marinade. Broil 15 to 20 minutes longer or until juice of chicken is clear when thickest part is cut to bone (170°F).

tip for *two*

For a pretty presentation, garnish with pitted ripe olives, cherry tomatoes and parsley.

1 Serving: Calories 340 (Calories from Fat 160); Total Fat 18g (Saturated Fat 4g; Trans Fat 0g); Cholesterol 115mg; Sodium 95mg; Total Carbohydrate 0g (Dietary Fiber 0g; Sugars 0g); Protein 42g **% Daily Value:** Vitamin A 4%; Vitamin C 0%; Calcium 4%; Iron 10% **Exchanges:** 6 Very Lean Meat, 3 Fat **Carbohydrate Choices:** 0

Grilled Pizza Chicken Kabobs

Prep Time: 35 minutes | **Start to Finish:** 35 minutes | 2 servings

3/4 lb uncooked chicken breast tenders (not breaded)

1/2 medium red bell pepper, cut into 1-inch pieces (1/2 cup)

1/2 package (8-oz size) fresh whole mushrooms

2 tablespoons reduced-fat Italian dressing

1 teaspoon pizza seasoning

2 tablespoons grated Parmesan cheese

1/4 cup pizza sauce (from 14-oz jar)

1 Heat gas or charcoal grill. On each of 2 (11-inch) metal skewers, thread chicken, bell pepper and mushrooms alternately, leaving 1/2-inch space between each piece. Brush kabobs with dressing; sprinkle with pizza seasoning.

2 Place kabobs on grill. Cover grill; cook over medium heat 9 to 11 minutes, turning once, until chicken is no longer pink in center. Immediately sprinkle with cheese.

3 Meanwhile, in 1-quart saucepan, heat pizza sauce over low heat. Serve kabobs with warm sauce.

tip for *two*

If you do not have pizza seasoning on hand, use 1 teaspoon Italian seasoning. Use any color of bell pepper.

1 Serving: Calories 240 (Calories from Fat 50); Total Fat 6g (Saturated Fat 1.5g; Trans Fat 0g); Cholesterol 80mg; Sodium 620mg; Total Carbohydrate 7g (Dietary Fiber 2g; Sugars 4g); Protein 41g **% Daily Value:** Vitamin A 15%; Vitamin C 40%; Calcium 8%; Iron 8% **Exchanges:** 1 Vegetable, 5 1/2 Very Lean Meat, 1/2 Fat **Carbohydrate Choices:** 1/2

Grilled Sweet-and-Sour Chicken Packets

Prep Time: 30 minutes | **Start to Finish:** 30 minutes | 2 servings

2 boneless skinless chicken breasts

1/4 cup sweet-and-sour sauce

1 can (8 oz) pineapple chunks, drained

1/2 medium bell pepper, cut into strips

1/4 small onion, cut into small wedges

1/4 cup chow mein noodles, if desired

1 Heat gas or charcoal grill. Cut 2 (18 × 12-inch) sheets of heavy-duty foil; spray with cooking spray. Place 1 chicken breast on center of each sheet. Top each with 1 tablespoon sweet-and-sour sauce and half of the pineapple, bell pepper and onion. Top with remaining sauce.

2 Bring up 2 sides of foil over chicken and vegetables so edges meet. Seal edges, making tight 1/2-inch fold; fold again, allowing space for heat circulation and expansion. Fold other sides to seal.

3 Place packets on grill. Cover grill; cook over medium heat 12 to 18 minutes, rotating packets 1/2 turn after 6 minutes, until juice of chicken is clear when center of thickest part is cut (170°F). To serve, cut large X across top of each packet; carefully fold back foil to allow steam to escape. Top with noodles.

tip for *two*

Using heavy-duty foil is important so the packets do not tear during grilling.

1 Serving: Calories 260 (Calories from Fat 45); Total Fat 5g (Saturated Fat 1g; Trans Fat 0g); Cholesterol 75mg; Sodium 180mg; Total Carbohydrate 26g (Dietary Fiber 2g; Sugars 22g); Protein 28g   **% Daily Value:** Vitamin A 4%; Vitamin C 30%; Calcium 4%; Iron 8%   **Exchanges:** 1/2 Fruit, 1 Other Carbohydrate, 4 Very Lean Meat, 1/2 Fat **Carbohydrate Choices:** 2

Grilled Apple- and Ginger-Glazed Chicken Breasts

Prep Time: 30 minutes | **Start to Finish:** 30 minutes | 2 servings

2 tablespoons teriyaki baste and glaze (from 12-oz bottle)

2 tablespoons apple jelly

1/2 teaspoon grated gingerroot

2 teaspoons chopped fresh cilantro

2 boneless skinless chicken breasts

1 Heat gas or charcoal grill. In 1-quart saucepan, mix teriyaki glaze, apple jelly and gingerroot. Heat to boiling, stirring constantly, until jelly is melted. Spoon half of the mixture into small bowl or custard cup; stir in cilantro. Set aside to serve with chicken.

2 Place chicken on grill. Cover grill; cook over medium heat 15 to 20 minutes, turning and brushing with apple-ginger mixture during last 10 minutes of grilling, until juice of chicken is clear when center of thickest part is cut (170°F). Serve with reserved apple-ginger mixture.

tip for *two*

Buy a larger piece of gingerroot than what you'll use for this recipe, then wrap up the rest of the unpeeled root and freeze until needed.

1 Serving: Calories 220 (Calories from Fat 35); Total Fat 4g (Saturated Fat 1g; Trans Fat 0g); Cholesterol 75mg; Sodium 480mg; Total Carbohydrate 19g (Dietary Fiber 0g; Sugars 14g); Protein 27g **% Daily Value:** Vitamin A 0%; Vitamin C 0%; Calcium 4%; Iron 8% **Exchanges:** 1 1/2 Other Carbohydrate, 4 Very Lean Meat **Carbohydrate Choices:** 1

Slow Cooker Heartland Pork Stew (page 138)

Cozy Casseroles

Chicken and Corn Enchiladas

Prep Time: 15 minutes | **Start to Finish:** 40 minutes | 2 servings (2 enchiladas each)

1 can (10 oz) mild enchilada sauce

1 cup shredded cooked chicken

1 cup frozen whole kernel corn (from 1-lb bag), thawed

1/2 cup shredded Monterey Jack cheese (2 oz)

1/4 teaspoon chili powder

4 corn tortillas (6 inch)

1 medium green onion, thinly sliced (1 tablespoon)

1 Heat oven to 350°F. Spray 8-inch square baking dish with cooking spray. Spread 1/2 cup of the enchilada sauce in baking dish. In large bowl, mix chicken, corn, 1/4 cup of the cheese and the chili powder. Reserve remaining enchilada sauce and cheese.

2 On microwavable plate, stack tortillas and cover with microwavable paper towel; microwave on High 20 seconds to soften. Place slightly less than 1/2 cup chicken mixture down middle of each tortilla. Roll up tortillas; place seam sides down in baking dish.

3 Pour remaining enchilada sauce over enchiladas. Sprinkle with remaining 1/4 cup cheese and the onion.

4 Bake uncovered 20 to 25 minutes or until cheese is melted and sauce is bubbly around edges.

tip for *two*

Shredded lettuce, avocado slices and chopped fresh cilantro are great extra toppers.

1 Serving: Calories 470 (Calories from Fat 160); Total Fat 18g (Saturated Fat 7g; Trans Fat 0g); Cholesterol 85mg; Sodium 930mg; Total Carbohydrate 45g (Dietary Fiber 5g; Sugars 6g); Protein 31g **% Daily Value:** Vitamin A 15%; Vitamin C 2%; Calcium 30%; Iron 10% **Exchanges:** 2 1/2 Starch, 1/2 Other Carbohydrate, 3 1/2 Very Lean Meat, 3 Fat **Carbohydrate Choices:** 3

Easy Baked Chicken and Potato Dinner

Prep Time: 20 minutes | **Start to Finish:** 1 hour | 2 servings

1/2 cup Heart Smart Bisquick® mix or Original Bisquick® mix

2 boneless skinless chicken breasts

2 tablespoons Dijon mustard

3/4 lb small red potatoes, cut into quarters

1 small red or green bell pepper, cut into 1/2-inch pieces

1 small onion, cut into 8 wedges

Cooking spray

2 tablespoons grated Parmesan cheese, if desired

1/2 teaspoon paprika

1 Heat oven to 400°F. Spray 13 × 9-inch (3-quart) glass baking dish with cooking spray.

2 Place Bisquick mix in shallow dish. Brush chicken with 1 tablespoon of the mustard, then coat with Bisquick mix. Place chicken breasts in baking dish at opposite ends. Place potatoes, bell pepper and onion in center of dish; brush vegetables with remaining mustard. Spray chicken and vegetables with cooking spray; sprinkle evenly with cheese and paprika.

3 Bake uncovered 35 to 40 minutes, stirring vegetables after 20 minutes, until potatoes are tender and juice of chicken is clear when center of thickest part is cut (170°F).

tip for two

Let your imagination and your taste buds run wild by trying different potatoes for color and flavor. Choose Yukon Gold, purple, yellow Finnish or Texas finger potatoes.

1 Serving: Calories 430 (Calories from Fat 70); Total Fat 8g (Saturated Fat 1.5g; Trans Fat 0g); Cholesterol 75mg; Sodium 770mg; Total Carbohydrate 58g (Dietary Fiber 6g; Sugars 7g); Protein 33g **% Daily Value:** Vitamin A 35%; Vitamin C 80%; Calcium 20%; Iron 30% **Exchanges:** 2 1/2 Starch, 1 Other Carbohydrate, 1 Vegetable, 3 Very Lean Meat, 1 Fat **Carbohydrate Choices:** 4

Chicken and Cornbread Stuffing Casserole

Prep Time: 15 minutes | **Start to Finish:** 30 minutes | 2 servings (about 1 1/2 cups each)

2/3 cup condensed 99%-fat-free cream of chicken or celery soup with 30% less sodium (from 10 3/4-oz can)

1/3 cup fat-free (skim) milk

1 cup frozen mixed vegetables (from 1-lb bag), thawed

1 small onion, finely chopped (1/4 cup)

1/4 teaspoon ground sage or poultry seasoning

1 cup cubed cooked chicken

3/4 cup cornbread stuffing mix

Dash pepper

Paprika, if desired

1 Heat oven to 400°F. Spray 1 1/2-quart casserole with cooking spray. In 2-quart saucepan, heat soup and milk to boiling over medium-high heat, stirring frequently. Stir in mixed vegetables, onion and sage. Heat to boiling, stirring frequently; remove from heat.

2 Stir in chicken and stuffing mix. Spoon into casserole. Sprinkle with pepper and paprika.

3 Bake uncovered about 15 minutes or until hot in center.

tip for *two*

The cream of chicken or celery soup is the base for this easy casserole. Use the remaining soup in another casserole, or freeze it to use when making this recipe another time.

1 Serving: Calories 350 (Calories from Fat 80); Total Fat 9g (Saturated Fat 2.5g; Trans Fat 0g); Cholesterol 65mg; Sodium 980mg; Total Carbohydrate 39g (Dietary Fiber 6g; Sugars 7g); Protein 28g **% Daily Value:** Vitamin A 90%; Vitamin C 4%; Calcium 10%; Iron 15% **Exchanges:** 1 1/2 Starch, 1/2 Other Carbohydrate, 1 Vegetable, 3 Lean Meat **Carbohydrate Choices:** 2 1/2

Slow Cooker Herbed Turkey and Wild Rice Casserole

Prep Time: 20 minutes | **Start to Finish:** 3 hours 35 minutes | 4 servings (1 2/3 cups each); 2 servings for planned-overs

4 slices bacon, cut into 1/2-inch pieces

3/4 lb turkey breast tenderloins, cut into 3/4-inch pieces

1 cup chopped celery

2/3 cup chopped carrot

1 medium onion, chopped (1/2 cup)

1 can (14 oz) reduced-sodium chicken broth

1/2 cup water

1/4 teaspoon dried marjoram leaves

1/4 teaspoon pepper

1 cup uncooked wild rice, rinsed, drained

1 can (10 3/4 oz) condensed 99% fat-free cream of chicken soup with 30% less sodium

1 In 12-inch skillet, cook bacon over medium heat, stirring occasionally, until crisp. Stir in turkey. Cook 3 to 5 minutes, stirring occasionally, until turkey is brown. Stir in celery, carrot and onion. Cook 2 minutes, stirring occasionally; drain.

2 In 3- to 3 1/2-quart slow cooker, mix turkey mixture and remaining ingredients except soup.

3 Cover; cook on Low heat setting 3 to 4 hours or until rice is tender and liquid is absorbed.

4 Stir in soup. Increase heat setting to High. Cover; cook 15 minutes longer or until mixture is hot.

tip for *two*

Marjoram adds an interesting herb flavor to this slow-cooked casserole. If you don't have it, you can use dried oregano leaves instead.

1 Serving: Calories 370 (Calories from Fat 60); Total Fat 6g (Saturated Fat 2g; Trans Fat 0g); Cholesterol 65mg; Sodium 790mg; Total Carbohydrate 46g (Dietary Fiber 4g; Sugars 4g); Protein 33g **% Daily Value:** Vitamin A 60%; Vitamin C 4%; Calcium 6%; Iron 15% **Exchanges:** 2 1/2 Starch, 1 Vegetable, 3 1/2 Very Lean Meat, 1/2 Fat **Carbohydrate Choices:** 3

5 easy Seasonings for Chicken and Turkey

Add zip to your chicken breasts or turkey breast tenderloins. Use a shake of your favorite seasoning to add a quick flavor hit.

1 Italian Seasoning

Sprinkle Italian seasoning on chicken or turkey before sautéing, then top cooked breasts with pizza sauce and shredded cheese and heat through.

2 Lemon-Herb

Rub chicken or turkey with lemon or lime juice, and sprinkle with your favorite chopped fresh herb, dried herb or herb blend.

3 Corn and Cajun/Creole

Mix Cajun or Creole seasoning with crushed corn flake crumbs, and coat chicken or turkey.

4 Garlic-Pepper or Lemon-Pepper

Sprinkle garlic-pepper blend or lemon-pepper seasoning on chicken or turkey, and sauté in olive oil with white wine.

5 Caribbean Jerk

Brush chicken or turkey with lime juice, and sprinkle with Caribbean jerk seasoning. Serve with salsa and fresh mango slices.

Slow Cooker Creole Jambalaya

Prep Time: 10 minutes | **Start to Finish:** 7 hours 40 minutes | 4 servings (about 1 cup each); 2 servings for planned-overs

2 medium stalks celery, chopped (1 cup)

4 cloves garlic, finely chopped

2 cans (14.5 oz each) diced tomatoes with green pepper and onion, undrained

1/2 cup chopped fully cooked smoked sausage

1/2 teaspoon dried thyme leaves

1/4 teaspoon pepper

1/4 teaspoon red pepper sauce

12 oz uncooked deveined peeled medium (26 to 30 count) shrimp, thawed if frozen, tail shells removed

2/3 cup uncooked long-grain white rice

1 1/3 cups water

1 In 3- to 3 1/2-quart slow cooker, mix all ingredients except shrimp, rice and water.

2 Cover; cook on Low heat setting 7 to 8 hours or until vegetables are tender.

3 Stir in shrimp. Cover; cook on Low heat setting about 30 minutes or until shrimp are pink. Meanwhile, cook rice in water as directed on package, omitting butter and salt. Serve jambalaya with rice.

tip for *two*

If you're trying to increase the amount of whole grains you eat, use brown rice in place of the white rice and follow the package directions for cooking.

1 Serving: Calories 300 (Calories from Fat 50); Total Fat 6g (Saturated Fat 2g; Trans Fat 0g); Cholesterol 130mg; Sodium 910mg; Total Carbohydrate 43g (Dietary Fiber 3g; Sugars 12g); Protein 19g   % Daily Value: Vitamin A 8%; Vitamin C 15%; Calcium 10%; Iron 25%   Exchanges: 1 1/2 Starch, 1 Other Carbohydrate, 1 Vegetable, 2 Lean Meat Carbohydrate Choices: 3

Southwest Tamale Tart

Prep Time: 15 minutes | **Start to Finish:** 40 minutes | 2 servings

1/2 cup Bisquick Heart Smart™ mix

1/4 cup cornmeal

3/4 cup shredded reduced-fat Cheddar cheese (3 oz)

1 tablespoon canned chopped green chiles, drained

3 tablespoons condensed beef broth

1 cup canned black beans, drained, rinsed

1/4 cup chopped fresh cilantro

1 small tomato, seeded, chopped (1/2 cup)

Salsa (any variety), if desired

Reduced-fat sour cream, if desired

Guacamole, if desired

1 Heat oven to 350°F. Spray cooking sheet with cooking spray.

2 In small bowl, stir Bisquick mix, cornmeal, 1/2 cup of the cheese and the chiles thoroughly. Stir in broth. Spread mixture in 7-inch circle on cookie sheet. In small bowl, mix beans and cilantro; spoon over cornmeal mixture to within 1/2 inch of edge. Sprinkle with remaining 1/4 cup cheese.

3 Bake 23 to 25 minutes or until edge is golden brown. Arrange tomatoes around edge of tart. Cut tart into wedges; serve with salsa, sour cream and guacamole.

tip for *two*

If you have beef broth remaining, freeze it in a clean ice-cube tray. Store the frozen broth cubes in a plastic freezer bag, and use in soups and stews. Pull one out to add extra flavor to meat dishes.

1 Serving: Calories 380 (Calories from Fat 50); Total Fat 6g (Saturated Fat 2g; Trans Fat 0g); Cholesterol 10mg; Sodium 920mg; Total Carbohydrate 59g (Dietary Fiber 7g; Sugars 7g); Protein 23g   **% Daily Value:** Vitamin A 15%; Vitamin C 6%; Calcium 50%; Iron 25%   **Exchanges:** 3 1/2 Starch, 1/2 Other Carbohydrate, 1 1/2 Very Lean Meat, 1/2 Fat **Carbohydrate Choices:** 4

Savory Beef Stew

Prep Time: 15 minutes | Start to Finish: 2 hours 15 minutes | 2 servings (2 cups each)

1/2 lb beef stew meat

10 ready-to-eat baby-cut carrots

4 small red potatoes (1/2 lb), cut in half

1/2 medium onion, cut into 4 wedges

1 can (14.5 oz) stewed tomatoes, undrained

1/8 teaspoon pepper

1 dried bay leaf

3/4 cup water

2 teaspoons all-purpose flour

1 Heat oven to 325°F. In 1 1/2-quart casserole, mix beef, carrots, potatoes, onion, tomatoes, pepper and bay leaf.

2 In small bowl, mix water and flour; stir into beef mixture.

3 Cover; bake about 2 hours, stirring once, until beef and vegetables are tender. Remove bay leaf.

tip for *two*

Add a bit of rich flavor, if you have the time, by browning the beef in a little oil before assembling the stew. Use small red potatoes that are firm and uniform size.

1 Serving: Calories 400 (Calories from Fat 130); Total Fat 14g (Saturated Fat 5g; Trans Fat 0.5g); Cholesterol 65mg; Sodium 690mg; Total Carbohydrate 44g (Dietary Fiber 6g; Sugars 16g); Protein 25g   **% Daily Value:** Vitamin A 120%; Vitamin C 30%; Calcium 10%; Iron 35%   **Exchanges:** 2 Starch, 2 Vegetable, 2 1/2 Medium-Fat Meat   **Carbohydrate Choices:** 3

Slow Cooker Mediterranean Minestrone Casserole

Prep Time: 20 minutes | **Start to Finish:** 6 hours 40 minutes | 4 servings (1 1/3 cups each); 2 servings for planned-overs

2 medium carrots, sliced (1 cup)

1 small onion, chopped (1/4 cup)

1 cup water

2 teaspoons sugar

1 teaspoon Italian seasoning

1/4 teaspoon pepper

1 can (28 oz) diced tomatoes, undrained

1 can (15 to 16 oz) garbanzo beans, drained, rinsed

1 can (6 oz) Italian-style tomato paste

2 cloves garlic, finely chopped

1 cup frozen cut green beans (from 1-lb bag), thawed

1 cup uncooked elbow macaroni (3 1/2 oz)

1/2 cup shredded Parmesan cheese (2 oz)

1 In 3- to 4-quart slow cooker, mix all ingredients except green beans, macaroni and cheese.

2 Cover; cook on Low heat setting 6 to 8 hours.

3 Stir in green beans and macaroni. Increase heat setting to High. Cover; cook about 20 minutes or until beans and macaroni are tender. Sprinkle with cheese.

tip for *two*

If you prefer, substitute a can of kidney or great northern beans for the garbanzo beans. Adding sugar, even a small amount, can balance the acid level of the tomatoes and round out the flavor.

1 Serving: Calories 450 (Calories from Fat 70); Total Fat 7g (Saturated Fat 3g; Trans Fat 0g); Cholesterol 10mg; Sodium 850mg; Total Carbohydrate 75g (Dietary Fiber 13g; Sugars 16g); Protein 22g **% Daily Value:** Vitamin A 100%; Vitamin C 25%; Calcium 35%; Iron 45% **Exchanges:** 3 Starch, 1 Other Carbohydrate, 3 Vegetable, 1 Very Lean Meat, 1 Fat **Carbohydrate Choices:** 5

Slow Cooker Heartland Pork Stew

Prep Time: 30 minutes | **Start to Finish:** 7 hours 45 minutes | 6 servings (1 cup each); 4 servings for planned-overs

2 lb boneless pork shoulder, cut into 1-inch pieces

1/2 teaspoon salt

1/4 teaspoon pepper

1 tablespoon canola oil

2 medium dark-orange sweet potatoes, peeled, cut into 2-inch pieces

1 box (9 oz) frozen baby lima beans

1 can (14 oz) reduced-sodium chicken broth

1/2 teaspoon salt

1/2 teaspoon dried thyme leaves

1/4 teaspoon dried sage leaves

1/4 cup water

2 tablespoons cornstarch

1 Sprinkle pork with 1/2 teaspoon salt and the pepper. In 12-inch skillet, heat oil over medium-high heat. Cook half of the pork in oil 5 to 8 minutes, stirring occasionally, until pork is brown; place in 3- to 4-quart slow cooker. Repeat with remaining pork.

2 Add sweet potatoes, frozen lima beans, broth, 1/2 teaspoon salt, the thyme and sage to pork in cooker.

3 Cover; cook on Low heat setting 7 to 8 hours.

4 In small bowl, mix water and cornstarch; stir into pork mixture. Increase heat setting to High. Cover; cook about 15 minutes or until mixture is thickened.

See photo on page 124

tip for *two*

To save time, cut the pork and sweet potatoes the night before. Wrap separately in plastic wrap or food-storage plastic bags and refrigerate.

1 Serving: Calories 420 (Calories from Fat 190); Total Fat 21g (Saturated Fat 7g; Trans Fat 0g); Cholesterol 95mg; Sodium 650mg; Total Carbohydrate 22g (Dietary Fiber 4g; Sugars 5g); Protein 37g **% Daily Value:** Vitamin A 200%; Vitamin C 15%; Calcium 4%; Iron 15% **Exchanges:** 1 1/2 Starch, 4 1/2 Lean Meat, 1 1/2 Fat **Carbohydrate Choices:** 1 1/2

Stuffed Pasta Shells

Prep Time: 30 minutes | **Start to Finish:** 55 minutes | 2 servings

6 uncooked jumbo pasta shells

1/4 lb ground turkey breast

1/2 teaspoon Italian seasoning

1/4 teaspoon fennel seed

1/8 teaspoon pepper

1 cup sliced fresh mushrooms

1 small onion, chopped (1/4 cup)

2 cloves garlic, finely chopped

1/2 cup reduced-fat cottage cheese

1 egg or 2 egg whites

1 cup tomato pasta sauce

2 tablespoons shredded Parmesan cheese

1 Heat oven to 350°F. Cook and drain pasta as directed on package, omitting salt.

2 Meanwhile, in 10-inch nonstick skillet, cook turkey, Italian seasoning, fennel seed and pepper over medium heat 8 to 10 minutes, stirring occasionally, until turkey is no longer pink; remove turkey mixture from skillet.

3 In same skillet, cook mushrooms, onion and garlic over medium heat 6 to 8 minutes, stirring occasionally, until vegetables are tender. Stir in turkey mixture, cottage cheese and egg.

4 Spray 8-inch square (2-quart) glass baking dish with cooking spray. Spoon about 1 tablespoon turkey mixture into each pasta shell. Place in baking dish. Spoon pasta sauce over shells.

5 Cover with foil. Bake 20 to 25 minutes or until hot. Sprinkle with Parmesan cheese.

tip for *two*

Look for a pasta sauce with a sodium content of 400 milligrams or less per serving. Balance the sodium with foods that contain potassium, like potatoes, bananas and other fruits and vegetables.

1 Serving: Calories 460 (Calories from Fat 120); Total Fat 14g (Saturated Fat 4.5g; Trans Fat 0g); Cholesterol 155mg; Sodium 1,030mg; Total Carbohydrate 51g (Dietary Fiber 4g; Sugars 16g); Protein 32g **% Daily Value:** Vitamin A 15%; Vitamin C 15%; Calcium 20%; Iron 20% **Exchanges:** 2 Starch, 1 Other Carbohydrate, 1 Vegetable, 3 1/2 Lean Meat, 1/2 Fat **Carbohydrate Choices:** 3 1/2

Macaroni and Cheese

Prep Time: 15 minutes | **Start to Finish:** 40 minutes | 2 servings (1 cup each)

1 cup uncooked elbow macaroni
(3 1/2 oz)

1 tablespoon butter or margarine

2 tablespoons all-purpose flour

1/4 teaspoon salt

1/8 teaspoon pepper

1/8 teaspoon ground mustard

1/8 teaspoon Worcestershire
sauce

1 cup fat-free (skim) milk

3/4 cup shredded reduced-fat
Cheddar cheese (3 oz)

1 Heat oven to 350°F. Cook and drain macaroni as directed on package.

2 Meanwhile, in 1-quart saucepan, melt butter over low heat. Stir in flour, salt, pepper, mustard and Worcestershire sauce. Cook over low heat, stirring constantly, until mixture is smooth and bubbly; remove from heat. Stir in milk. Heat to boiling over medium-low heat, stirring constantly. Boil and stir 1 minute; remove from heat. Stir in cheese until melted.

3 Gently stir macaroni into cheese sauce. Pour into ungreased 1-quart casserole.

4 Bake uncovered 20 to 25 minutes or until bubbly.

tip for *two*

Add surprise to your mac and cheese by mixing cheeses! Try Jarlsberg®, smoked Gouda or white Cheddar. Stir in crumbled cooked bacon, and whole wheat pasta for a hearty, richly flavored twist.

1 Serving: Calories 440 (Calories from Fat 90); Total Fat 10g (Saturated Fat 6g; Trans Fat 0g); Cholesterol 25mg; Sodium 1,050mg; Total Carbohydrate 63g (Dietary Fiber 4g; Sugars 8g); Protein 24g   **% Daily Value:** Vitamin A 10%; Vitamin C 0%; Calcium 45%; Iron 15%   **Exchanges:** 3 Starch, 1 Other Carbohydrate, 2 Medium-Fat Meat **Carbohydrate Choices:** 4

Italian Pizza Bake

Prep Time: 15 minutes | **Start to Finish:** 40 minutes | 2 servings

1/3 cup Bisquick Heart Smart™ mix

1 egg white

1 tablespoon water

1/8 teaspoon garlic powder

1/4 cup diced green or yellow bell pepper

1/4 cup chopped onion

1/2 cup cut-up cooked chicken breast

1/2 cup drained diced tomatoes with Italian herbs (from 14.5-oz can)

1/4 teaspoon Italian seasoning

1/4 cup shredded mozzarella cheese (1 oz)

1 Heat oven to 400°F. Spray 8 × 4-inch loaf pan with cooking spray. In small bowl, mix Bisquick mix, egg white, water and garlic powder; spread in pan.

2 In 10-inch nonstick skillet, cook bell pepper and onion over medium-high heat, stirring frequently, until onion is tender. Stir in chicken, tomatoes and Italian seasoning; cook until thoroughly heated. Spoon over batter in pan. Sprinkle with cheese.

3 Bake 20 to 23 minutes or until golden brown; loosen from sides of pan.

tip for *two*

When you need only a small amount of cooked chicken breast, it's handy to just purchase one piece of cooked chicken from the grocery store deli. Remove the skin and bone, and you will have about 1 cup of chicken.

1 Serving: Calories 200 (Calories from Fat 50); Total Fat 6g (Saturated Fat 2.5g; Trans Fat 0g); Cholesterol 35mg; Sodium 420mg; Total Carbohydrate 20g (Dietary Fiber 1g; Sugars 5g); Protein 18g   **% Daily Value:** Vitamin A 4%; Vitamin C 20%; Calcium 20%; Iron 10%   **Exchanges:** 1/2 Starch, 1/2 Other Carbohydrate, 1 Vegetable, 2 Very Lean Meat, 1 Fat   **Carbohydrate Choices:** 1

Baked Pork Chops and Vegetables

Prep Time: 15 minutes | **Start to Finish:** 1 hour 10 minutes | 2 servings

2 pork loin chops, 1/2 inch thick (about 6 oz each)

1/8 teaspoon garlic-pepper blend

1 cup frozen diced hash brown potatoes (from 32-oz bag), thawed

1/2 cup frozen mixed vegetables (from 1-lb bag), thawed

2/3 cup condensed 98% fat-free cream of celery soup (from 10 3/4-oz can)

1/4 cup chive-and-onion sour cream potato topper

1/8 teaspoon dried thyme leaves

1/2 cup Parmesan-flavored croutons, coarsely crushed

1 Heat oven to 350°F. Spray 8-inch square (2-quart) glass baking dish with cooking spray. Sprinkle pork chops with garlic-pepper blend.

2 Heat 10-inch nonstick skillet over medium-high heat. Cook pork in skillet 4 to 6 minutes or until browned on both sides. Place pork in baking dish. In medium bowl, mix potatoes, vegetables, soup, sour cream potato topper and thyme. Spoon over pork chops.

3 Cover baking dish with foil. Bake 30 minutes. Sprinkle with croutons; press into mixture slightly. Bake uncovered 20 to 25 minutes longer or until bubbly and pork is no longer pink when cut near bone.

tip for *two*

Pressed for time? Although browning adds extra flavor, you can omit the step and instead just season the chops and place in the baking dish.

1 Serving: Calories 450 (Calories from Fat 160); Total Fat 17g (Saturated Fat 7g; Trans Fat 0g); Cholesterol 85mg; Sodium 850mg; Total Carbohydrate 41g (Dietary Fiber 5g; Sugars 6g); Protein 33g   **% Daily Value:** Vitamin A 50%; Vitamin C 10%; Calcium 10%; Iron 15%   **Exchanges:** 2 Starch, 1/2 Other Carbohydrate, 4 Lean Meat, 1 Fat **Carbohydrate Choices:** 3

Bacon-Chili Beef Stew

Prep Time: 35 minutes | **Start to Finish:** 1 hour 50 minutes | 2 servings (1 1/2 cups each)

2 slices bacon, cut into 1/2-inch pieces

1/2 lb beef stew meat (1/2-inch pieces)

1 small onion, chopped (1/4 cup)

Dash pepper

1 can (8 oz) no-salt-added tomato sauce

1/2 cup home-style beef gravy (from 12-oz jar)

1 tablespoon chili sauce

2 unpeeled small red potatoes, diced (1 cup)

1 medium carrot, sliced (1/2 cup)

1/2 cup frozen whole kernel corn (from 1-lb bag)

1 In 2-quart nonstick saucepan, cook bacon over medium heat 3 to 4 minutes, stirring frequently, until cooked but not crisp.

2 Stir beef and onion into bacon. Sprinkle with pepper. Cook 4 to 6 minutes, stirring frequently, until beef begins to brown and onion is tender.

3 Stir in tomato sauce, gravy and chili sauce. Heat to boiling. Add potatoes and carrot. Cover; cook over medium-low heat 50 to 60 minutes, stirring occasionally, until beef is tender.

4 Stir in corn. Cook uncovered 10 to 15 minutes longer, stirring occasionally, until corn is tender.

tip for *two*

Like your chili spicy? Use tomatoes labeled "zesty" instead of the mild variety.

1 Serving: Calories 450 (Calories from Fat 170); Total Fat 19g (Saturated Fat 7g; Trans Fat 0.5g); Cholesterol 75mg; Sodium 720mg; Total Carbohydrate 39g (Dietary Fiber 6g; Sugars 10g); Protein 31g   **% Daily Value:** Vitamin A 80%; Vitamin C 25%; Calcium 6%; Iron 30%   **Exchanges:** 1 Starch, 1 1/2 Other Carbohydrate, 1 Vegetable, 3 1/2 Medium-Fat Meat   **Carbohydrate Choices:** 2 1/2

Easy Chicken and Garden Veggies (page 148)

Fast Skillet Meals

Easy Chicken and Garden Veggies

Prep Time: 35 minutes | **Start to Finish:** 35 minutes | 2 servings

2 slices bacon, cut into 1/2-inch pieces

2 boneless skinless chicken breasts

1/4 teaspoon garlic salt

1/8 teaspoon coarsely ground pepper

2 tablespoons water

4 oz fresh green beans, trimmed (leave whole)

1/2 medium yellow bell pepper, cut into 1/2-inch pieces

1 medium plum (Roma) tomato, cut lengthwise in half, then sliced (about 1/3 cup)

1/4 cup fat-free balsamic vinaigrette dressing or fat-free Italian dressing

1 In 10-inch nonstick skillet, cook bacon over medium heat 3 to 4 minutes, stirring occasionally, until crisp. Remove bacon from skillet; keep warm.

2 Sprinkle both sides of chicken with garlic salt and pepper. Place chicken in skillet. Cook 3 to 5 minutes or until browned on both sides. Discard excess bacon drippings.

3 Add water and green beans to skillet. Cover; cook over medium-low heat 8 minutes. Stir in bell pepper. Cover; cook 3 to 5 minutes, turning and stirring vegetables occasionally, until juice of chicken is clear when center of thickest part is cut (170°F).

4 Stir in tomato and dressing. Cook uncovered about 2 minutes, stirring occasionally, until tomato is thoroughly heated. Sprinkle with cooked bacon.

See photo on page 146

tip for *two*

The plum tomatoes hold their shape when cooked briefly and don't add a lot of extra liquid to the vegetables. You can use frozen whole green beans instead of the fresh, if you like.

1 Serving: Calories 230 (Calories from Fat 70); Total Fat 7g (Saturated Fat 2g; Trans Fat 0g); Cholesterol 80mg; Sodium 840mg; Total Carbohydrate 10g (Dietary Fiber 2g; Sugars 6g); Protein 31g   **% Daily Value:** Vitamin A 10%; Vitamin C 50%; Calcium 4%; Iron 10%   **Exchanges:** 1/2 Other Carbohydrate, 1 Vegetable, 4 Very Lean Meat, 1 Fat **Carbohydrate Choices:** 1/2

Caesar Chicken with Orzo

| Prep Time: 30 minutes | Start to Finish: 30 minutes | 2 servings |

1 teaspoon canola oil

2 boneless skinless chicken breasts

1 cup reduced-sodium chicken broth

1/2 cup water

1/2 cup uncooked orzo or rosamarina pasta

1/2 bag (1-lb size) frozen broccoli cuts

1/2 medium red bell pepper, cut into strips

2 teaspoons reduced-fat Caesar dressing

Dash coarsely ground pepper

1 In 10-inch skillet, heat oil over medium-high heat. Cook chicken in oil about 10 minutes, turning once, until brown on both sides. Remove chicken from skillet; keep warm.

2 Carefully add broth and water to hot skillet; heat to boiling. Stir in pasta; heat to boiling. Cook uncovered 8 to 10 minutes, stirring occasionally. Stir in broccoli, bell pepper and dressing (cut any large broccoli pieces in half).

3 Add chicken to pasta mixture; sprinkle with pepper. Heat to boiling; reduce heat. Simmer uncovered about 5 minutes or until vegetables are crisp-tender and juice of chicken is clear when center of thickest part is cut (170°F).

tip for *two*

People often think orzo is rice because of its shape and size. It actually is pasta, and because it is small, it cooks very quickly. Serve this easy meal with a tossed lettuce and tomato wedge salad topped with your favorite dressing.

1 Serving: Calories 340 (Calories from Fat 60); Total Fat 7g (Saturated Fat 1.5g; Trans Fat 0g); Cholesterol 75mg; Sodium 410mg; Total Carbohydrate 34g (Dietary Fiber 5g; Sugars 4g); Protein 36g   % Daily Value: Vitamin A 40%; Vitamin C 80%; Calcium 6%; Iron 20%   Exchanges: 2 Starch, 1 Vegetable, 4 Very Lean Meat, 1/2 Fat   Carbohydrate Choices: 2

Buffalo-Style Turkey Tenderloin

Prep Time: 25 minutes | **Start to Finish:** 25 minutes | 2 servings

1 teaspoon olive oil

1/2 lb turkey breast tenderloin

1 cup refrigerated cooked new potato wedges (from 20-oz bag)

1 medium onion, chopped (1/2 cup)

1/2 medium red bell pepper, chopped (1/2 cup)

2 tablespoons reduced-fat blue cheese dressing

1 to 3 teaspoons cayenne pepper sauce

Chopped fresh parsley, if desired

1 In 12-inch nonstick skillet, heat oil over medium-low heat. Add turkey; cover and cook 10 minutes, turning after 5 minutes.

2 Add potatoes, onion and bell pepper to turkey. Cook uncovered about 5 minutes longer, stirring occasionally and adding 1 to 2 tablespoons water if needed, until juice of turkey is clear when center of thickest part is cut (170°F) and potatoes are tender.

3 Meanwhile, in small bowl, mix dressing and pepper sauce. Pour sauce over turkey mixture, stirring to coat. Reduce heat to low. Cook until sauce is thoroughly heated. Sprinkle with parsley.

tip for *two*

The heat and amount of flavor of pepper sauce vary by brand. The original cayenne pepper sauce has a sweeter flavor that is perfect for this buffalo-style entrée.

1 Serving: Calories 230 (Calories from Fat 40); Total Fat 4.5g (Saturated Fat 1g; Trans Fat 0g); Cholesterol 75mg; Sodium 340mg; Total Carbohydrate 17g (Dietary Fiber 4g; Sugars 6g); Protein 30g   **% Daily Value:** Vitamin A 25%; Vitamin C 60%; Calcium 4%; Iron 10%   **Exchanges:** 1/2 Starch, 1/2 Other Carbohydrate, 4 Very Lean Meat, 1/2 Fat **Carbohydrate Choices:** 1

Glazed Lemon Chicken and Rice

Prep Time: 20 minutes | **Start to Finish:** 20 minutes | 2 servings

1/3 cup water

1 tablespoon lemon juice

2 teaspoons cornstarch

2 tablespoons honey

1 teaspoon grated lemon peel

1 cup uncooked instant white rice

1 cup water

1 teaspoon olive oil

1/2 lb boneless skinless chicken breasts, cut into 1-inch pieces

1/2 teaspoon salt

3 green onions, cut into 1-inch pieces

1 small orange bell pepper, cut into 1-inch pieces

1 In 2-cup measuring cup, stir 1/3 cup water, the lemon juice, cornstarch, honey and lemon peel until cornstarch is dissolved; set aside.

2 Cook rice in 1 cup water as directed on package, omitting butter and salt; keep warm.

3 Meanwhile, in 10-inch nonstick skillet, heat oil over medium-high heat. Add chicken; sprinkle with salt. Cook 2 to 3 minutes, stirring frequently, until chicken is brown. Stir in onions and bell pepper. Cook 2 to 4 minutes, stirring frequently, until chicken is no longer pink in center. Reduce heat to low.

4 Stir lemon juice mixture in measuring cup. Pour into skillet; stir to coat chicken mixture. Cook until slightly thickened. Serve chicken mixture over rice.

tip for two

Purchase chicken breast tenders (unbreaded) for a quick alternative to boneless skinless chicken breasts. Garnish with a sprig of parsley and a lemon twist.

1 Serving: Calories 460 (Calories from Fat 60); Total Fat 6g (Saturated Fat 1.5g; Trans Fat 0g); Cholesterol 70mg; Sodium 660mg; Total Carbohydrate 71g (Dietary Fiber 2g; Sugars 20g); Protein 30g   **% Daily Value:** Vitamin A 8%; Vitamin C 60%; Calcium 6%; Iron 20%   **Exchanges:** 3 Starch, 1 1/2 Other Carbohydrate, 3 Very Lean Meat, 1/2 Fat **Carbohydrate Choices:** 5

Sauerbraten Meatballs

Prep Time: 30 minutes | **Start to Finish:** 55 minutes | 2 servings

MEATBALLS

1/2 lb extra-lean (at least 90%) ground beef

2 tablespoons finely crushed gingersnap cookies

2 tablespoons red wine vinegar

1/8 teaspoon salt

1/8 teaspoon pepper

1 small onion, finely chopped (1/4 cup)

1 egg white

NOODLES

2 1/2 cups uncooked egg noodles (4 oz)

SAUERBRATEN SAUCE

1/4 cup finely crushed gingersnap cookies

2 tablespoons raisins

1 tablespoon packed brown sugar

3/4 cup reduced-sodium beef broth

1 tablespoon red wine vinegar

1 Heat oven to 400°F. In small bowl, mix all meatball ingredients. Shape mixture into 10 (1 1/2-inch) meatballs. Place in ungreased 13 × 9-inch pan. Bake 20 to 25 minutes or until thoroughly cooked and no longer pink in center; drain.

2 Meanwhile, cook and drain noodles as directed on package, omitting salt.

3 In 2-quart saucepan, heat all sauce ingredients to boiling, stirring occasionally; reduce heat to medium. Cook 5 minutes, stirring occasionally, until thickened.

4 Stir drained meatballs into sauce. Serve over noodles.

tip for *two*

These authentic meatballs are easy to make and have a wonderful flavor. Try mixing things up a bit—for a change, you can serve them with brown rice or whole wheat couscous.

1 Serving: Calories 540 (Calories from Fat 130); Total Fat 14g (Saturated Fat 5g; Trans Fat 1g); Cholesterol 115mg; Sodium 440mg; Total Carbohydrate 71g (Dietary Fiber 3g; Sugars 25g); Protein 33g   **% Daily Value:** Vitamin A 0%; Vitamin C 0%; Calcium 6%; Iron 30%   **Exchanges:** 3 Starch, 1 1/2 Other Carbohydrate, 3 1/2 Lean Meat, 1/2 Fat **Carbohydrate Choices:** 5

Raspberry-Glazed Chicken

Prep Time: 25 minutes | **Start to Finish:** 25 minutes | 2 servings

2 teaspoons canola oil

2 boneless skinless chicken breasts

3 tablespoons raspberry jam

1 teaspoon Dijon mustard

1/2 cup fresh or frozen (thawed and drained) raspberries

1 In 10-inch nonstick skillet, heat oil over medium heat. Cook chicken in oil 15 to 20 minutes, turning once, until juice of chicken is clear when center of thickest part is cut (170°F).

2 In small bowl, mix jam and mustard. Spoon jam mixture over chicken; top with raspberries.

tip for *two*

Use seedless raspberry jam to make a smooth glaze; a mini whisk works well to quickly combine the raspberry jam and mustard.

1 Serving: Calories 290 (Calories from Fat 80); Total Fat 9g (Saturated Fat 1.5g; Trans Fat 0g); Cholesterol 75mg; Sodium 140mg; Total Carbohydrate 25g (Dietary Fiber 2g; Sugars 16g); Protein 27g   **% Daily Value:** Vitamin A 0%; Vitamin C 10%; Calcium 2%; Iron 8%   **Exchanges:** 1 1/2 Other Carbohydrate, 4 Very Lean Meat, 1 1/2 Fat **Carbohydrate Choices:** 1 1/2

5 *easy* Ready-in-a-Minute Sides

Maybe you've chosen your meat for a meal but can't think of a side dish to go with it. Try any one of these super-quick sides for ideas.

1 Sweet Potato Topper

Mix 1 tablespoon molasses, 1/4 teaspoon ground cinnamon and 2 tablespoons orange juice; pour over baked sweet potatoes.

2 Crunchy Winter Squash

Sprinkle toasted chopped soy nuts, almonds, peanuts or walnuts over baked acorn or butternut squash or sweet potatoes.

3 Creamy Quinoa or Couscous

Stir a bit of soft cream cheese and grated Romano or Parmesan cheese into cooked quinoa or couscous.

4 Lemon Rice

Stir grated lemon or lime peel and lemon or lime juice into cooked brown or white rice.

5 Orange- or Lemon-Glazed Vegetables

Stir melted butter, orange or lemon juice, grated orange or lemon peel, ground ginger and salt into cooked carrots, green beans or pea pods.

Margarita Shrimp Stir-Fry

Prep Time: 15 minutes | Start to Finish: 45 minutes | 2 servings

1/2 cup frozen (thawed) margarita mix

1 teaspoon grated lime peel

1/2 lb uncooked deveined peeled medium (26 to 30 count) shrimp, thawed if frozen, tail shells removed

1 tablespoon butter or margarine

1/2 medium green bell pepper, cut into thin strips

1/2 medium red bell pepper, cut into thin strips

1 tablespoon finely chopped cilantro

1 cup uncooked instant white rice

1 cup water

1 In small bowl, stir margarita mix and lime peel. Reserve 2 tablespoons mixture. Add shrimp to remaining mixture; toss to coat. Cover and refrigerate 30 minutes to marinate.

2 In 10-inch nonstick skillet, melt butter over medium-high heat. Cook green and red bell peppers in butter 2 to 4 minutes, stirring occasionally, until crisp-tender.

3 Remove shrimp from marinade; discard marinade. Stir shrimp into mixture in skillet. Cook 1 to 2 minutes, stirring occasionally, until shrimp are pink. Stir in reserved 2 tablespoons sauce and the cilantro. Cook until heated through.

4 Meanwhile, cook rice in water as directed on package, omitting butter and salt. Serve stir-fry over rice.

tip for two

Chicken is a great substitute for shrimp. Cut 1/2 pound of boneless skinless chicken breasts into 1-inch pieces; cook until no longer pink in the center. Try basmati or jasmine rice—start the rice before you cook the peppers, preparing as directed on the package.

1 Serving: Calories 390 (Calories from Fat 70); Total Fat 7g (Saturated Fat 4g; Trans Fat 0g); Cholesterol 175mg; Sodium 230mg; Total Carbohydrate 58g (Dietary Fiber 2g; Sugars 10g); Protein 22g   **% Daily Value:** Vitamin A 30%; Vitamin C 70%; Calcium 6%; Iron 25%   **Exchanges:** 3 Starch, 1/2 Other Carbohydrate, 1 Vegetable, 1 1/2 Very Lean Meat, 1 Fat   **Carbohydrate Choices:** 4

Seafood Frittata

Prep Time: 30 minutes | **Start to Finish:** 30 minutes | 2 servings

1 teaspoon olive oil

4 oz fresh asparagus, cut into 2-inch pieces (about 1 cup)

3/4 cup thinly sliced fresh mushrooms

1/2 cup chopped imitation crabmeat

4 eggs

1 teaspoon chopped fresh chives

1/4 cup shredded mozzarella cheese (1 oz)

1 Brush oil over bottom and up side of 10-inch nonstick skillet; heat over medium-low heat. Cook asparagus and mushrooms in skillet 3 to 4 minutes, stirring occasionally, until asparagus is crisp-tender. Reduce heat to medium-low. Stir in imitation crabmeat. Cook until thoroughly heated.

2 Spread mixture evenly in skillet. In small bowl, beat eggs and chives until well blended; pour evenly over asparagus mixture (do not stir). Cook 6 to 8 minutes or until egg is almost set. Sprinkle with cheese.

3 Set oven control to broil. Cover skillet handle with foil. Broil frittata with top 4 to 6 inches from heat 1 to 2 minutes or until cheese is melted and eggs are set. Cut in half; serve immediately.

tip for *two*

You can reduce the amount of cholesterol in this recipe by using egg product substitute instead of the eggs. Any fresh fruit slices make a quick, colorful accompaniment.

1 Serving: Calories 270 (Calories from Fat 150); Total Fat 16g (Saturated Fat 5g; Trans Fat 0g); Cholesterol 440mg; Sodium 500mg; Total Carbohydrate 6g (Dietary Fiber 1g; Sugars 3g); Protein 24g   **% Daily Value:** Vitamin A 25%; Vitamin C 10%; Calcium 15%; Iron 10%   **Exchanges:** 1 Vegetable, 3 Medium-Fat Meat   **Carbohydrate Choices:** 1/2

Corn Flake–Crusted Fish Fillets with Dilled Tartar Sauce

Prep Time: 30 minutes | **Start to Finish:** 30 minutes | 2 servings

1/4 cup fat-free mayonnaise (do not use salad dressing)

2 teaspoons finely chopped onion

1 tablespoon dill pickle relish

1/4 cup all-purpose flour

1 egg or 2 egg whites

1 tablespoon water

1 1/2 cups Country® Corn Flakes cereal, crushed (about 3/4 cup)

3/4 lb cod fillets, cut into 2 serving pieces

1 tablespoon canola oil

1 In small bowl, mix mayonnaise, onion and pickle relish. Cover; refrigerate.

2 Meanwhile, in shallow dish, place flour. In another shallow dish, beat egg and water with fork. Place crushed cereal in third shallow dish. Dip fish in flour, coating well; shake off excess. Dip floured fish in egg mixture, then in cereal, coating all sides completely.

3 In 10-inch nonstick skillet, heat oil over medium heat until hot. Cook fish in oil 6 to 8 minutes, turning once, until well browned and fish flakes easily with fork.

4 Serve fish topped with sauce.

tip for *two*

Please your sweet-pickle-relish lovers by adding relish to the tartar sauce instead of the dill pickle relish. Instead of making the tartar sauce from scratch, buy your favorite brand.

1 Serving: Calories 410 (Calories from Fat 120); Total Fat 13g (Saturated Fat 2.5g; Trans Fat 0g); Cholesterol 200mg; Sodium 730mg; Total Carbohydrate 36g (Dietary Fiber 2g; Sugars 5g); Protein 38g **% Daily Value:** Vitamin A 10%; Vitamin C 4%; Calcium 25%; Iron 40% **Exchanges:** 2 Starch, 1/2 Other Carbohydrate, 4 1/2 Very Lean Meat, 1 1/2 Fat **Carbohydrate Choices:** 2 1/2

Penne with Spicy Sauce

Prep Time: 25 minutes | Start to Finish: 25 minutes | 2 servings (2 1/4 cups each)

2 cups uncooked penne pasta
(6 oz)

1 tablespoon olive oil

1 clove garlic, finely chopped

1/2 teaspoon crushed red pepper
flakes

1 tablespoon chopped fresh
parsley

1 can (14.5 oz) diced tomatoes,
undrained

1 tablespoon tomato paste

1/4 cup freshly grated or
shredded Parmesan cheese (1 oz)

1 Cook and drain pasta as directed on package, omitting salt.

2 In 10-inch skillet, heat oil over medium-high heat. Cook garlic, red pepper and parsley in oil about 5 minutes, stirring frequently, until garlic just begins to turn golden. Stir in tomatoes and tomato paste. Heat to boiling; reduce heat. Cover; simmer about 10 minutes, stirring occasionally, until slightly thickened.

3 Add pasta and 2 tablespoons of the cheese to tomato mixture. Cook about 3 minutes, tossing gently, until pasta is evenly coated. Sprinkle with remaining 2 tablespoons cheese.

tip for *two*

Tame the fiery pepper flakes with steamed broccoli and French bread. If you'd like a glass of wine, try Chianti.

1 Serving: Calories 490 (Calories from Fat 110); Total Fat 12g (Saturated Fat 3.5g; Trans Fat 0g); Cholesterol 10mg; Sodium 560mg; Total Carbohydrate 77g (Dietary Fiber 7g; Sugars 8g); Protein 18g   **% Daily Value:** Vitamin A 15%; Vitamin C 20%; Calcium 25%; Iron 35%   **Exchanges:** 4 Starch, 1/2 Other Carbohydrate, 2 Vegetable, 2 Fat **Carbohydrate Choices:** 5

Chicken Fried Steak with Country Gravy

Prep Time: 40 minutes | **Start to Finish:** 40 minutes | 2 servings

STEAKS

2 tablespoons all-purpose flour

1/4 teaspoon seasoned salt

1/4 teaspoon pepper

1 egg or 2 egg whites

1 tablespoon fat-free (skim) milk

9 saltine crackers, finely crushed (1/3 cup)

2 beef cube steaks (4 oz each)

1 teaspoon canola oil

GRAVY

2 teaspoons canola oil

1 tablespoon all-purpose flour

2/3 cup fat-free (skim) milk

1 teaspoon beef bouillon granules

1/8 teaspoon pepper

1 In shallow dish, mix 2 tablespoons flour, the seasoned salt and 1/4 teaspoon pepper. In another shallow dish, beat egg and 1 tablespoon milk with fork. Place cracker crumbs on a sheet of waxed paper.

2 Dip beef steaks in flour mixture, coating well; shake off excess. Dip floured beef in egg mixture, then in cracker crumbs, turning to coat completely; shake off excess.

3 In 10-inch nonstick skillet, heat 1 teaspoon oil over low heat until hot. Cook beef in oil 10 to 12 minutes, turning once, until golden brown. Place steaks on plate; cover to keep warm while making gravy.

4 Add 2 teaspoons oil to same skillet. Stir in 1 tablespoon flour, scraping up brown particles. Cook over medium-high heat 2 to 3 minutes, stirring constantly, until mixture is light golden brown. Stir in 2/3 cup milk, the bouillon granules and 1/8 teaspoon pepper. Heat over medium-high heat, stirring constantly, until mixture is boiling and thickened. If gravy is too thick, stir in more milk, 1 tablespoon at a time, until desired consistency. Spoon gravy over steaks.

1 Serving: Calories 400 (Calories from Fat 170); Total Fat 19g (Saturated Fat 4.5g; Trans Fat 1g); Cholesterol 155mg; Sodium 830mg; Total Carbohydrate 23g (Dietary Fiber 0g; Sugars 7g); Protein 35g   **% Daily Value:** Vitamin A 6%; Vitamin C 0%; Calcium 15%; Iron 20%   **Exchanges:** 1 Starch, 1/2 Other Carbohydrate, 4 1/2 Lean Meat, 1 Fat **Carbohydrate Choices:** 1 1/2

Sesame Stir-Fry

Prep Time: 20 minutes | **Start to Finish:** 20 minutes | 2 servings

1 cup water

Dash salt

1/2 cup uncooked instant brown rice

2 tablespoons reduced-sodium soy sauce

1 teaspoon lemon juice

2 teaspoons cornstarch

1/2 teaspoon toasted sesame oil

1 teaspoon canola oil

1/2 lb uncooked chicken breast tenders (not breaded), pieces cut in half lengthwise

1 1/2 cups frozen bell pepper and onion stir-fry (from 1-lb bag), thawed, drained

1/2 teaspoon sesame seed

1 In 1-quart saucepan, heat 2/3 cup of the water and the salt to boiling over high heat. Stir in rice. Reduce heat to low. Cover; simmer about 10 minutes or until water is absorbed. Fluff with fork.

2 Meanwhile, in small bowl, stir remaining 1/3 cup water, the soy sauce, lemon juice, cornstarch and sesame oil; set aside.

3 Heat nonstick wok or 10-inch skillet over medium-high heat. Add canola oil; rotate wok to coat side. Add chicken; stir-fry 2 to 3 minutes. Add stir-fry vegetables; stir-fry 3 to 5 minutes or until chicken is no longer pink in center and vegetables are crisp-tender.

4 Stir soy sauce mixture into chicken mixture; heat to boiling. Cook and stir until sauce is thickened. Sprinkle with sesame seed. Serve with rice.

tip for *two*

Other combinations of frozen vegetables can be substituted for the stir-fry vegetables. Use your favorite.

1 Serving: Calories 300 (Calories from Fat 50); Total Fat 5g (Saturated Fat 0g; Trans Fat 0g); Cholesterol 50mg; Sodium 750mg; Total Carbohydrate 34g (Dietary Fiber 3g; Sugars 5g); Protein 28g   **% Daily Value:** Vitamin A 4%; Vitamin C 35%; Calcium 2%; Iron 6%   **Exchanges:** 2 Starch, 1 Vegetable, 3 Very Lean Meat, 1/2 Fat   **Carbohydrate Choices:** 2

Szechuan Chicken and Pasta

Prep Time: 30 minutes | **Start to Finish:** 30 minutes | 2 servings

1/2 lb boneless skinless chicken breasts, cut into 3/4- to 1-inch pieces

1/2 small red onion, cut into thin wedges

1 cup water

3/4 cup uncooked fusilli pasta (about 3 oz)

1/2 bag (1 lb 5 oz-size) frozen Szechuan stir-fry mix with vegetables and Szechuan sauce

1 Spray 10-inch nonstick skillet with cooking spray; heat over medium-high heat. Add chicken and onion; stir-fry 3 to 5 minutes or until chicken is light brown.

2 Stir in water; heat to boiling. Stir in pasta. Cook 8 to 10 minutes, stirring occasionally, until pasta is almost tender (do not drain).

3 Stir in packet of sauce mix from stir-fry mix until well blended. Stir in vegetables; reduce heat to medium. Cover; cook 8 to 9 minutes, stirring occasionally, until vegetables are crisp-tender. Sprinkle with peanuts from stir-fry mix.

tip for two

For an additional time-saver, look for already-sliced chicken breast strips in the meat aisle (the package may be labeled "chicken for stir-fry"). You'll need about 1/2 pound of strips for this recipe.

1 Serving: Calories 350 (Calories from Fat 40); Total Fat 4.5g (Saturated Fat 1g; Trans Fat 0g); Cholesterol 70mg; Sodium 820mg; Total Carbohydrate 44g (Dietary Fiber 5g; Sugars 5g); Protein 33g   **% Daily Value:** Vitamin A 30%; Vitamin C 25%; Calcium 6%; Iron 20%   **Exchanges:** 2 Starch, 1/2 Other Carbohydrate, 1 Vegetable, 3 1/2 Very Lean Meat **Carbohydrate Choices:** 3

Maple-Mustard Pork

Prep Time: 20 minutes | **Start to Finish:** 20 minutes | 2 servings

1/2 lb pork tenderloin

2 tablespoons all-purpose flour

1/8 teaspoon salt

2 teaspoons canola oil

3 tablespoons water

1 tablespoon real maple syrup

1 tablespoon Dijon mustard

1 Cut pork crosswise in half. Between pieces of plastic wrap or waxed paper, place each pork piece with cut side up; gently pound with flat side of meat mallet or rolling pin until about 1/4 inch thick.

2 In shallow dish, mix flour and salt. Coat pork with flour mixture.

3 In 10-inch nonstick skillet, heat oil over medium-high heat. Cook pork in oil 4 to 5 minutes on each side or until golden brown on outside and no longer pink in center. Remove from skillet; cover to keep warm.

4 In small bowl, beat water, maple syrup and mustard with wire whisk. Add to skillet; cook and stir about 1 minute or until slightly thickened. Serve sauce over pork.

tip for *two*

Try other varieties of mustard, such as spicy brown mustard or regular yellow mustard.

1 Serving: Calories 250 (Calories from Fat 90); Total Fat 9g (Saturated Fat 2g; Trans Fat 0g); Cholesterol 70mg; Sodium 390mg; Total Carbohydrate 13g (Dietary Fiber 0g; Sugars 6g); Protein 27g   **% Daily Value:** Vitamin A 0%; Vitamin C 0%; Calcium 0%; Iron 10%   **Exchanges:** 1/2 Starch, 1/2 Other Carbohydrate, 3 1/2 Very Lean Meat, 1 1/2 Fat **Carbohydrate Choices:** 1

Mediterranean Salmon-Pasta Toss

Prep Time: 25 minutes | **Start to Finish:** 25 minutes | 2 servings

4 oz uncooked linguine

2 teaspoons olive oil

6 oz skinless salmon fillet, cut into 1-inch pieces

1/2 cup sliced fresh mushrooms

6 asparagus spears, cut into 1-inch pieces

1 clove garlic, finely chopped

2 tablespoons chopped fresh basil or 1 teaspoon dried basil leaves

6 grape tomatoes

1 medium green onion, sliced (1 tablespoon)

2 teaspoons cornstarch

1/2 cup reduced-sodium chicken broth

2 tablespoons shredded Parmesan cheese

1 Cook and drain linguine as directed on package, omitting salt.

2 Meanwhile, in 10-inch nonstick skillet, heat oil over medium heat. Cook salmon in oil 4 to 5 minutes, stirring gently and frequently, until salmon flakes easily with fork (salmon may break apart). Remove from skillet.

3 Increase heat to medium-high. Add mushrooms, asparagus and garlic to skillet; cook and stir 2 minutes. Stir in basil, tomatoes and onion; cook and stir 1 minute longer.

4 In 2-cup glass measuring cup, stir cornstarch into broth. Add to vegetable mixture. Cook and stir 1 to 2 minutes or until sauce is thickened and bubbly. Stir in salmon. Serve over linguine. Sprinkle with cheese.

tip for *two*

Cherry tomatoes can be used instead of the grape variety. Just cut 3 cherry tomatoes in half and continue as directed.

1 Serving: Calories 440 (Calories from Fat 110); Total Fat 13g (Saturated Fat 3.5g; Trans Fat 0g); Cholesterol 60mg; Sodium 310mg; Total Carbohydrate 51g (Dietary Fiber 5g; Sugars 3g); Protein 31g **% Daily Value:** Vitamin A 15%; Vitamin C 15%; Calcium 15%; Iron 20% **Exchanges:** 3 Starch, 1 Vegetable, 3 Lean Meat, 1/2 Fat **Carbohydrate Choices:** 3 1/2

Peppers Stuffed with Broccoli, Beans and Rice

Prep Time: 20 minutes | **Start to Finish:** 35 minutes | 2 servings

2 large bell peppers, cut in half lengthwise, seeded

2/3 cup water

1/2 cup uncooked instant brown rice

1 cup chopped fresh broccoli

2 tablespoons chopped onion

1/2 cup canned red beans, drained, rinsed

1/3 cup chunky-style salsa

1/4 cup shredded reduced-fat Cheddar cheese (1 oz)

2 tablespoons chopped fresh cilantro

1 In 8- or 9-inch square microwavable dish, place peppers, cut sides down. Cover dish with plastic wrap, folding back one edge or corner 1/4 inch to vent steam. Microwave on High about 4 minutes or until tender.

2 Meanwhile, in 1-quart saucepan, heat water to boiling over high heat. Stir in rice, broccoli and onion; reduce heat to low. Cover; simmer about 10 minutes or until water is absorbed. Stir in beans and salsa.

3 Spoon hot rice mixture into pepper halves. Place filled sides up in microwavable dish. Sprinkle each pepper half with 1 tablespoon of the cheese. Cover dish with plastic wrap, folding back one edge or corner 1/4 inch to vent steam. Microwave on High about 1 minute or until cheese is melted. Sprinkle with cilantro. Let stand 1 to 2 minutes before serving.

tip for *two*

Indulge yourself in colorful red, yellow or orange bell peppers instead of green. Not only do they retain their cheerful color, they add more sweetness than green bell peppers do.

1 Serving: Calories 250 (Calories from Fat 20); Total Fat 2.5g (Saturated Fat 1g; Trans Fat 0g); Cholesterol 0mg; Sodium 340mg; Total Carbohydrate 45g (Dietary Fiber 9g; Sugars 7g); Protein 13g   **% Daily Value:** Vitamin A 30%; Vitamin C 130%; Calcium 15%; Iron 15%   **Exchanges:** 2 Starch, 1/2 Other Carbohydrate, 1 1/2 Vegetable, 1/2 Lean Meat **Carbohydrate Choices:** 3

Skillet Cheddar Bread (page 178)

Small Batch Baking

Orange-Honey Dinner Rolls

Prep Time: 5 minutes | **Start to Finish:** 15 minutes | 2 servings

2 teaspoons honey

1/2 teaspoon grated orange peel

2 frozen crusty French dinner rolls (from 12.4-oz package)

1 Heat oven to 425°F. In small bowl, mix honey and orange peel.

2 Bake rolls as directed on package. Immediately after removing rolls from oven, brush tops with honey mixture. Serve immediately.

tip for *two*

Having guests over for dinner? This recipe can easily be doubled or tripled.

1 Serving: Calories 130 (Calories from Fat 15); Total Fat 1.5g (Saturated Fat 0g; Trans Fat 0g); Cholesterol 0mg; Sodium 200mg; Total Carbohydrate 24g (Dietary Fiber 0g; Sugars 8g); Protein 4g   **% Daily Value:** Vitamin A 0%; Vitamin C 0%; Calcium 0%; Iron 6%   **Exchanges:** 1 1/2 Starch   **Carbohydrate Choices:** 1 1/2

Grilled Herbed Stuffed Bread

Prep Time: 15 minutes | **Start to Finish:** 15 minutes | 2 servings

1 oz reduced-fat cream cheese (Neufchâtel), softened

1/8 teaspoon Italian seasoning

Dash garlic salt

2 crusty dinner rolls (4 inches long), cut in half crosswise

1 Heat gas or charcoal grill for indirect heat as directed by manufacturer. Cut 2 (12 × 8-inch) sheets of heavy-duty foil.

2 In small bowl, mix cream cheese, Italian seasoning and garlic salt. Spread on cut sides of rolls. Place each roll on center of foil sheet. Bring up 2 sides of foil over roll so edges meet. Seal edges, making tight 1/2-inch fold; fold again, allowing space for heat circulation and expansion. Fold other sides to seal.

3 Place packets on grill for indirect cooking. Cover grill; cook over medium heat 7 to 10 minutes or until rolls are thoroughly heated.

tip for *two*

The cream cheese mixture can be made up to 4 hours in advance and refrigerated; spread it on the rolls when you are ready to grill. If you want to grill these rolls along with your entrée, start 15 minutes before your entrée is done.

1 Serving: Calories 140 (Calories from Fat 45); Total Fat 5g (Saturated Fat 2g; Trans Fat 0g); Cholesterol 10mg; Sodium 290mg; Total Carbohydrate 18g (Dietary Fiber 0g; Sugars 2g); Protein 5g **% Daily Value:** Vitamin A 4%; Vitamin C 0%; Calcium 0%; Iron 6% **Exchanges:** 1 Starch, 1/2 High-Fat Meat **Carbohydrate Choices:** 1

Skillet Cheddar Bread

Prep Time: 10 minutes | Start to Finish: 30 minutes | 4 servings

3/4 cup all-purpose flour

2 tablespoons instant nonfat dry milk

2 teaspoons sugar

1/2 teaspoon cream of tartar

1/4 teaspoon baking soda

1/8 teaspoon salt

2 tablespoons firm butter (do not use margarine)

1/4 cup shredded reduced-fat Cheddar cheese (1 oz)

1/3 cup water

1/2 teaspoon canola oil

1 In medium bowl, mix flour, dry milk, sugar, cream of tartar, baking soda and salt. Cut in butter, using pastry blender (or pulling 2 table knives through ingredients in opposite directions), until mixture looks like cornmeal. Gently stir in cheese. Stir in water just until dough forms (do not overmix).

2 In 8-inch nonstick skillet, brush oil in bottom and up side. Press dough into 1/2-inch-thick round. Cut into 4 wedges. Place wedges in skillet; cover with foil.

3 Cook over low heat about 10 minutes or until puffed and bottoms are light brown. Turn wedges; cook about 10 minutes longer or until cooked through.

See photo on page 172

tip for two

No need to heat your oven for this tasty bread—it "bakes" in your skillet and is a snap to stir together. Tightly wrap remaining wedges and chill or freeze for another time.

1 Serving: Calories 170 (Calories from Fat 60); Total Fat 7g (Saturated Fat 4g; Trans Fat 0g); Cholesterol 15mg; Sodium 270mg; Total Carbohydrate 21g (Dietary Fiber 0g; Sugars 3g); Protein 5g   **% Daily Value:** Vitamin A 4%; Vitamin C 0%; Calcium 8%; Iron 6%   **Exchanges:** 1 1/2 Starch, 1 Fat   **Carbohydrate Choices:** 1 1/2

Sesame Wedges

Prep Time: 5 minutes | **Start to Finish:** 20 minutes | 6 wedges

1 cup Bisquick Heart Smart™ mix

1/4 cup water

1 tablespoon butter or margarine, melted

1 tablespoon sesame seed

1 Heat oven to 400°F. Spray cookie sheet with cooking spray.

2 In small bowl, stir Bisquick mix and water with fork until soft dough forms. Pat dough into 7-inch circle on cookie sheet. Brush with butter. Sprinkle with sesame seed; press firmly into dough with rubber spatula. Cut dough into 6 wedges.

3 Bake 10 to 15 minutes or until golden brown. Serve warm.

tip for *two*

Personalize this quick bread by sprinkling 2 tablespoons chopped fresh or 2 teaspoons dried basil or sage leaves on the top before baking to create irresistible aromas and flavors. Freeze remaining servings for another time.

1 Wedge: Calories 100 (Calories from Fat 35); Total Fat 4g (Saturated Fat 1.5g; Trans Fat 0g); Cholesterol 5mg; Sodium 230mg; Total Carbohydrate 14g (Dietary Fiber 0g; Sugars 2g); Protein 2g   **% Daily Value:** Vitamin A 0%; Vitamin C 0%; Calcium 8%; Iron 4%   **Exchanges:** 1 Starch, 1/2 Fat   **Carbohydrate Choices:** 1

Petite Orange and Cream Scones

Prep Time: 15 minutes | **Start to Finish:** 40 minutes | 4 scones

3/4 cup all-purpose flour

2 1/2 teaspoons sugar

1/2 teaspoon baking powder

Dash salt

2 tablespoons firm butter
(do not use margarine)

1/4 cup white vanilla baking chips

1/2 teaspoon grated orange peel

1 egg or 2 egg whites, beaten

2 tablespoons fat-free
half-and-half

1 Heat oven to 400°F. In small bowl, mix flour, sugar, baking powder and salt. Cut in butter, using pastry blender (or pulling 2 table knives through ingredients in opposite directions), until mixture looks like coarse crumbs. Stir in 2 tablespoons of the baking chips, the orange peel, egg and half-and-half until soft dough forms.

2 On lightly floured surface, knead dough about 5 seconds or until dough is smooth. Pat dough into a round, 1/2 inch thick. Cut round into 4 wedges.

3 On ungreased cookie sheet, place wedges 1 inch apart. Bake 12 to 15 minutes or until light golden brown. Remove from cookie sheet to cooling rack; cool 10 minutes.

4 In small microwavable bowl, place remaining 2 tablespoons baking chips. Microwave uncovered on High 1 minute; stir until chips are smooth. Place melted chips in resealable food-storage plastic bag; seal. Cut off tiny corner of bag; squeeze to drizzle melted chips over scones. Serve warm.

tip for *two*

Scones are best served warm. To reheat scones, microwave one at a time on a microwavable plate on High 15 to 20 seconds until warm.

1 Scone: Calories 250 (Calories from Fat 100); Total Fat 11g (Saturated Fat 7g; Trans Fat 0g); Cholesterol 70mg; Sodium 200mg; Total Carbohydrate 31g (Dietary Fiber 0g; Sugars 12g); Protein 5g   **% Daily Value:** Vitamin A 6%; Vitamin C 0%; Calcium 8%; Iron 8%   **Exchanges:** 1 1/2 Starch, 1/2 Other Carbohydrate, 2 Fat   **Carbohydrate Choices:** 2

Easy Garlic-Cheese Biscuits

Prep Time: 10 minutes | **Start to Finish:** 20 minutes | 5 biscuits

1 cup Bisquick Heart Smart™ mix

1/3 cup fat-free (skim) milk

1/4 cup shredded reduced-fat Cheddar cheese (1 oz)

1 tablespoon butter, melted (do not use margarine)

1/8 teaspoon garlic powder

1 Heat oven to 450°F. In small bowl, stir Bisquick mix, milk and cheese with wire whisk or fork until soft dough forms; beat vigorously 30 seconds.

2 Onto ungreased cookie sheet, drop dough by 5 spoonfuls about 2 inches apart.

3 Bake 8 to 10 minutes or until golden brown. In small bowl, stir butter and garlic powder until well mixed; brush on warm biscuits before removing from cookie sheet. Serve warm.

tip for *two*

To make Easy Herb-Cheese Biscuits, stir in 1/4 to 1/2 teaspoon dried dill weed, dried rosemary leaves (crushed) or Italian seasoning with the Bisquick mix.

1 Biscuit: Calories 120 (Calories from Fat 40); Total Fat 4g (Saturated Fat 1.5g; Trans Fat 0g); Cholesterol 10mg; Sodium 340mg; Total Carbohydrate 17g (Dietary Fiber 0g; Sugars 3g); Protein 4g   **% Daily Value:** Vitamin A 2%; Vitamin C 0%; Calcium 15%; Iron 6%   **Exchanges:** 1 Starch, 1 Fat   **Carbohydrate Choices:** 1

1 Handheld Immersion Blender

A handheld blender whips and blends. It's much smaller than a regular blender. Use for sauces, drinks, smoothies and smooth soups.

2 Compact Indoor Grill

This kitchen helper heats fast, cooks food quickly, is easy to clean and tucks easily into a cupboard for storage. It's ideal for cooking 1 or 2 servings of meat, vegetables, or sandwiches.

3 Mini Food Chopper

A handy tool, perfect for two people. It is small enough to leave on your counter, processes small amounts of food with ease and is perfect for chopping a small onion, nuts, herbs, vegetables and more.

4 Toaster Oven

Designed to mount under a cabinet, it leaves your counter free. Most models bake and broil. Two pork chops, 2 or 3 pieces of garlic bread, 2 individual pizzas, small amounts of anything bake well in a toaster oven.

5 Small Slow Cookers

Slow cookers that are 1- to 1 1/2-quart size are great for hot dips and spreads and are a good size for 2 or 3 portions of food. They work well for 2 or 3 pork chops, a pound of chicken thighs or 3 to 4 cups of soup or stew.

5 easy Kitchen Appliances

Make your life easy in a small kitchen.

Buttermilk Cornbread

Prep Time: 15 minutes | **Start to Finish:** 40 minutes | 6 servings

3/4 cup yellow, white or blue cornmeal

1/4 cup all-purpose flour

1/4 cup sugar

3/4 cup low-fat buttermilk

2 tablespoons canola oil

1/2 teaspoon baking powder

1/2 teaspoon salt

1/2 teaspoon baking soda

1 egg or 2 egg whites

1 Heat oven to 450°F. Spray bottom only of 8 × 4-inch loaf pan with cooking spray. In medium bowl, mix all ingredients with spoon until well mixed. Beat vigorously 30 seconds. Pour into pan.

2 Bake 20 to 25 minutes or until toothpick inserted in center comes out clean. Serve warm.

tip for *two*

This cornbread has extra flavor from the buttermilk and is great served with chili or soup. Since it makes 6 servings, eat a couple now and freeze the rest.

1 Serving: Calories 180 (Calories from Fat 60); Total Fat 6g (Saturated Fat 1g; Trans Fat 0g); Cholesterol 40mg; Sodium 380mg; Total Carbohydrate 28g (Dietary Fiber 0g; Sugars 10g); Protein 4g   **% Daily Value:** Vitamin A 2%; Vitamin C 0%; Calcium 8%; Iron 6%   **Exchanges:** 1 1/2 Starch, 1/2 Other Carbohydrate, 1 Fat   **Carbohydrate Choices:** 2

Ginger-Carrot-Nut Bread

| **Prep Time:** 15 minutes | **Start to Finish:** 1 hour 35 minutes | 2 small loaves (6 slices each) |

1 egg or 2 egg whites

1/3 cup packed brown sugar

2 tablespoons canola oil

1/4 cup fat-free (skim) milk

1/2 teaspoon vanilla

1 cup all-purpose flour

1 teaspoon baking powder

1/2 teaspoon ground ginger

1/4 teaspoon salt

1/2 cup shredded carrot
(about 1 medium)

1/4 cup chopped nuts

1 Heat oven to 350°F. Grease bottoms only of 2 (5 × 3-inch) disposable loaf pans with shortening; lightly flour (or spray bottom of pan with cooking spray; do not flour).

2 In medium bowl, beat egg and brown sugar with electric mixer on medium speed until creamy. Beat in oil, milk and vanilla. Beat in flour, baking powder, ginger and salt until smooth. Stir in carrot and nuts. Spread in pans.

3 Bake 35 to 40 minutes or until toothpick inserted in center comes out clean. Cool in pans 10 minutes; remove from pans to cooling rack. Cool completely, about 30 minutes, before slicing.

tip for *two*

The disposable loaf pans in your grocery store are perfect for baking small loaves of bread. This carrot-nut bread makes two small loaves; serve one now and wrap the other one tightly and freeze.

1 Slice: Calories 110 (Calories from Fat 40); Total Fat 4.5g (Saturated Fat 0g; Trans Fat 0g); Cholesterol 20mg; Sodium 60mg; Total Carbohydrate 15g (Dietary Fiber 0g; Sugars 7g); Protein 2g   **% Daily Value:** Vitamin A 10%; Vitamin C 0%; Calcium 0%; Iron 4%   **Exchanges:** 1/2 Starch, 1/2 Other Carbohydrate, 1 Fat   **Carbohydrate Choices:** 1

Raspberry-Chocolate Muffins

Prep Time: 15 minutes | **Start to Finish:** 40 minutes | 6 muffins

2/3 cup Fiber One® cereal

2/3 cup low-fat buttermilk

2 tablespoons canola oil

1 egg or 2 egg whites

1/2 cup all-purpose flour

1/3 cup sugar

2 tablespoons unsweetened baking cocoa

1 teaspoon baking soda

1/8 teaspoon salt

1/3 cup fresh or frozen (thawed and drained) raspberries

1 Heat oven to 375°F. Place paper baking cup in each of 6 regular-size muffin cups. Place cereal in food-storage plastic bag or between sheets of waxed paper; crush with rolling pin (or crush in blender or food processor).

2 In medium bowl, stir crushed cereal and buttermilk; let stand 5 minutes. Stir in oil and egg. Stir in flour, sugar, cocoa, baking soda and salt until moistened. Gently stir in raspberries. Divide batter evenly among muffin cups.

3 Bake 20 to 25 minutes or until toothpick inserted in center comes out clean. Immediately remove from pan.

tip for *two*

Combining the popular tastes of chocolate and raspberry, these fantastic muffins are packed with fiber, the part of plant foods your body cannot digest. Fiber helps keep you regular and may help reduce your cholesterol. These muffins keep a couple of days at room temperature, or freeze the rest to eat later.

1 Muffin: Calories 190 (Calories from Fat 60); Total Fat 7g (Saturated Fat 1g; Trans Fat 0g); Cholesterol 40mg; Sodium 320mg; Total Carbohydrate 28g (Dietary Fiber 4g; Sugars 13g); Protein 4g **% Daily Value:** Vitamin A 0%; Vitamin C 2%; Calcium 8%; Iron 10% **Exchanges:** 1 1/2 Starch, 1/2 Other Carbohydrate, 1 Fat **Carbohydrate Choices:** 2

Sweet Potato–Oat Muffins

Prep Time: 20 minutes | Start to Finish: 40 minutes | 6 muffins

1/4 cup old-fashioned or quick-cooking oats

1/2 cup low-fat buttermilk

1 egg or 2 egg whites, beaten

2 tablespoons packed brown sugar

2 tablespoons butter, melted (do not use margarine)

1/3 cup finely shredded peeled sweet potato

3/4 cup all-purpose flour

1/2 teaspoon baking soda

1/4 teaspoon salt

1/4 teaspoon ground cinnamon

2 teaspoons old-fashioned or quick-cooking oats

1 tablespoon granulated sugar

1/8 teaspoon ground cinnamon

1 Heat oven to 400°F. Place paper baking cup in each of 6 regular-size muffin cups; spray paper cups with cooking spray. Or grease bottoms only of 6 regular-size muffin cups with shortening or cooking spray.

2 In medium bowl, mix 1/4 cup oats and the buttermilk with fork; let stand 5 minutes. Stir in egg, brown sugar, butter and sweet potato. Add flour, baking soda, salt and 1/4 teaspoon cinnamon; stir just until dry ingredients are moistened. Divide batter evenly among muffin cups (3/4 full).

3 In small bowl, mix 2 teaspoons oats, the granulated sugar and 1/8 teaspoon cinnamon. Sprinkle over batter in each cup.

4 Bake 15 to 20 minutes or until toothpick inserted in center comes out clean. Immediately remove from pan to cooling rack. Serve warm.

tip for *two*

You can substitute the same amount of shredded carrot for the sweet potato. These muffins keep well at room temperature for a couple of days or can be frozen. To reheat, microwave on High for 15 to 20 seconds until warm.

1 Muffin: Calories 160 (Calories from Fat 50); Total Fat 6g (Saturated Fat 3g; Trans Fat 0g); Cholesterol 45mg; Sodium 260mg; Total Carbohydrate 24g (Dietary Fiber 1g; Sugars 8g); Protein 4g   **% Daily Value:** Vitamin A 30%; Vitamin C 0%; Calcium 4%; Iron 6%   **Exchanges:** 1 Starch, 1/2 Other Carbohydrate, 1 Fat   **Carbohydrate Choices:** 1 1/2

Triple-Strawberry Sundaes (page 195)

Indulgent Desserts

Pineapple and Berries with Honey-Mint Topping

Prep Time: 15 minutes | **Start to Finish:** 15 minutes | 2 servings (3/4 cup each)

2 tablespoons frozen (thawed) lemonade concentrate

1 tablespoon honey

1 teaspoon chopped fresh mint leaves

1/4 fresh pineapple, peeled, cored and cut into chunks (about 1 cup)

2 tablespoons fresh blueberries

2 tablespoons fresh raspberries

2 tablespoons sliced fresh strawberries

1 In small bowl, mix lemonade concentrate, honey and mint.

2 In another small bowl, gently stir together remaining ingredients. Stir in lemonade mixture until fruits are coated. Serve immediately, or refrigerate up to 4 hours.

tip for *two*

You can buy fresh pineapple chunks in the refrigerated fruit section of most grocery stores. Go berry crazy and use any combination of your favorite berries!

1 Serving: Calories 130 (Calories from Fat 0); Total Fat 0g (Saturated Fat 0g; Trans Fat 0g); Cholesterol 0mg; Sodium 0mg; Total Carbohydrate 30g (Dietary Fiber 2g; Sugars 25g); Protein 0g **% Daily Value:** Vitamin A 0%; Vitamin C 70%; Calcium 0%; Iron 2% **Exchanges:** 1/2 Fruit, 1 1/2 Other Carbohydrate **Carbohydrate Choices:** 2

Cran-Pear Crisp

Prep Time: 5 minutes | **Start to Finish:** 45 minutes | 2 servings

2 medium pears, peeled, sliced

1 teaspoon lemon juice

1 tablespoon dried cranberries

1 tablespoon packed brown sugar

1 tablespoon butter or margarine, melted

4 gingersnap cookies, crushed

1 Heat oven to 375°F. Spray 1-quart casserole with cooking spray. Place pears in casserole; sprinkle with lemon juice.

2 In small bowl, mix remaining ingredients until crumbly; sprinkle over pears.

3 Cover; bake 30 to 40 minutes or until pears are tender.

tip for *two*

Using on-hand cookies is an easy way to make a crisp. The strong flavor of the ginger-snaps is a nice complement to the mild pears.

1 Serving: Calories 260 (Calories from Fat 70); Total Fat 7g (Saturated Fat 4g; Trans Fat 0.5g); Cholesterol 15mg; Sodium 125mg; Total Carbohydrate 46g (Dietary Fiber 6g; Sugars 32g); Protein 1g   **% Daily Value:** Vitamin A 4%; Vitamin C 6%; Calcium 2%; Iron 4%   **Exchanges:** 1 Fruit, 2 Other Carbohydrate, 1 1/2 Fat   **Carbohydrate Choices:** 3

Triple-Strawberry Sundaes

Prep Time: 10 minutes | **Start to Finish:** 10 minutes | 2 servings

1 cup strawberry reduced-fat frozen yogurt

8 medium strawberries, sliced

1/4 cup strawberry topping

2 tablespoons granola

1 Divide yogurt between 2 dessert dishes. Top with strawberries.

2 Pour strawberry topping over strawberries and yogurt. Sprinkle with granola.

See photo on page 190

tip for *two*

Easy and pretty, this dessert feels indulgent. For variety, use vanilla ice cream or frozen yogurt as well as different flavors of granola bars, crushed up, for the granola.

1 Serving: Calories 300 (Calories from Fat 30); Total Fat 3.5g (Saturated Fat 2g; Trans Fat 0g); Cholesterol 5mg; Sodium 95mg; Total Carbohydrate 61g (Dietary Fiber 2g; Sugars 47g); Protein 7g **% Daily Value:** Vitamin A 0%; Vitamin C 50%; Calcium 20%; Iron 4% **Exchanges:** 1 Starch, 3 Other Carbohydrate, 1/2 Low-Fat Milk **Carbohydrate Choices:** 4

Baked Apples with Rum-Caramel Sauce

Prep Time: 5 minutes | **Start to Finish:** 15 minutes | 2 servings

2 medium baking apples

1 tablespoon water

1/2 cup vanilla reduced-fat ice cream

1/4 cup caramel topping

2 teaspoons rum or apple cider

Dash ground cinnamon

1 Cut thin slice off bottom and top of each apple. Using paring knife or apple corer, remove core from each apple.

2 In 8- or 9-inch square microwavable dish, place apples upright. Pour 1 tablespoon water over apples. Cover with microwavable plastic wrap, folding back one edge or corner 1/4 inch to vent steam. Microwave on High 8 to 10 minutes or until apples are tender.

3 Place apples in individual serving bowls; reserve 1 teaspoon cooking liquid. Cut each apple in half. For each serving, spoon 1/4 cup ice cream between apple halves. In small bowl, stir caramel topping, 1 teaspoon cooking liquid and the rum; pour over apples. Sprinkle with cinnamon.

tip for *two*

For a slightly different dessert, omit the ice cream and instead top each serving with a crunchy granola bar, crushed, and a dollop of fat-free whipped topping.

1 Serving: Calories 260 (Calories from Fat 25); Total Fat 3g (Saturated Fat 1.5g; Trans Fat 0g); Cholesterol 10mg; Sodium 170mg; Total Carbohydrate 55g (Dietary Fiber 4g; Sugars 42g); Protein 2g   **% Daily Value:** Vitamin A 6%; Vitamin C 6%; Calcium 8%; Iron 0%   **Exchanges:** 1 Fruit, 2 1/2 Other Carbohydrate, 1 Fat   **Carbohydrate Choices:** 3 1/2

Bananas Foster with Ice Cream

Prep Time: 10 minutes | **Start to Finish:** 10 minutes | 2 servings (1/2 cup ice cream and 1/2 cup banana mixture each)

1/4 cup caramel topping

**1 teaspoon dark rum or
1/2 teaspoon rum extract**

1 banana, sliced

1 cup vanilla reduced-fat ice cream

1 In small microwavable bowl, microwave caramel topping and rum uncovered on High 15 seconds or until very warm. Stir in banana.

2 Scoop ice cream into dessert dishes; top with banana mixture.

tip for *two*

This recipe is a lower-fat twist on the original version from Brennan's Restaurant in New Orleans. Use medium-ripe bananas for the best texture and flavor.

1 Serving: Calories 300 (Calories from Fat 50); Total Fat 5g (Saturated Fat 3.5g; Trans Fat 0g); Cholesterol 25mg; Sodium 200mg; Total Carbohydrate 58g (Dietary Fiber 2g; Sugars 41g); Protein 4g   **% Daily Value:** Vitamin A 8%; Vitamin C 4%; Calcium 10%; Iron 0%   **Exchanges:** 1 Fruit, 2 1/2 Other Carbohydrate, 1/2 Low-Fat Milk, 1/2 Fat **Carbohydrate Choices:** 4

Cherry Cobblers for Two

Prep Time: 5 minutes | **Start to Finish:** 25 minutes | 2 servings

1 cup cherry pie filling (from 21-oz can)

1/2 cup Bisquick Heart Smart™ mix

3 tablespoons fat-free (skim) milk

1 tablespoon sugar

1 teaspoon butter or margarine, softened

1 Heat oven to 400°F. Divide pie filling between 2 ungreased 10-ounce custard cups.

2 In small bowl, stir remaining ingredients until thick batter forms. Pour and spread half onto pie filling in each custard cup. Sprinkle with additional sugar if desired.

3 Bake 15 to 18 minutes or until topping is light brown.

tip for *two*

Extra pie filling? It makes a great topper for ice cream, pancakes, waffles and French toast.

1 Serving: Calories 300 (Calories from Fat 35); Total Fat 4g (Saturated Fat 1.5g; Trans Fat 0g); Cholesterol 5mg; Sodium 350mg; Total Carbohydrate 62g (Dietary Fiber 2g; Sugars 40g); Protein 4g **% Daily Value:** Vitamin A 4%; Vitamin C 6%; Calcium 15%; Iron 8% **Exchanges:** 1 Starch, 3 Other Carbohydrate, 1/2 Fat **Carbohydrate Choices:** 4

Rhubarb Oven Pudding

Prep Time: 15 minutes | **Start to Finish:** 45 minutes | 2 servings

**4 teaspoons butter
(do not use margarine)**

1/3 cup all-purpose flour

1/2 cup fat-free (skim) milk

1 egg or 2 egg whites

1/8 teaspoon salt

**3/4 cup frozen cut rhubarb
(from 16-oz bag), thawed, drained
and finely chopped**

1/3 cup packed brown sugar

1/4 teaspoon ground nutmeg

1 Heat oven to 425°F. In each of 2 (10-oz) custard cups, place 2 teaspoons butter. Heat in oven until bubbling.

2 Meanwhile, in small bowl, beat flour, milk, egg and salt with wire whisk just until smooth. Pour mixture into bubbling butter. Sprinkle rhubarb over batter. In small bowl, mix brown sugar and nutmeg; sprinkle over batter and rhubarb. Place cups in 11 × 7-inch glass baking dish.

3 Bake 20 to 25 minutes or until puffed and golden brown. Serve warm.

tip for *two*

You'll agree with the taste testers in the Betty Crocker Kitchens—this rhubarb pudding is scrumptious! Serve with frozen (thawed) fat-free whipped topping or reduced-fat frozen yogurt.

1 Serving: Calories 460 (Calories from Fat 100); Total Fat 11g (Saturated Fat 6g; Trans Fat 0g); Cholesterol 130mg; Sodium 270mg; Total Carbohydrate 83g (Dietary Fiber 2g; Sugars 65g); Protein 8g **% Daily Value:** Vitamin A 10%; Vitamin C 2%; Calcium 25%; Iron 10% **Exchanges:** 2 Starch, 3 1/2 Other Carbohydrate, 2 Fat **Carbohydrate Choices:** 5 1/2

Double-Chocolate Snack Cake

Prep Time: 10 minutes | **Start to Finish:** 1 hour 10 minutes | 6 servings

3/4 cup all-purpose flour

1/2 cup packed brown sugar

2 tablespoons unsweetened baking cocoa

1/2 teaspoon baking soda

1/4 teaspoon salt

1/2 cup water

3 tablespoons canola oil

1/2 teaspoon white vinegar

1/4 teaspoon vanilla

1/4 cup semisweet chocolate chips

Powdered sugar, if desired

1 Heat oven to 350°F. In ungreased 9 × 5-inch loaf pan, mix flour, brown sugar, cocoa, baking soda and salt with fork. Stir in remaining ingredients except chocolate chips and powdered sugar. Sprinkle chocolate chips over batter.

2 Bake 25 to 30 minutes or until toothpick inserted in center comes out clean. Cool in pan on cooling rack 30 minutes. Sprinkle with powdered sugar.

tip for *two*

This one-pan cake takes the work out of baking and adds back the fun. Since it makes more than you may need at one time, keep it stored in an airtight container at room temperature for up to three days or freeze for up to three months.

1 Serving: Calories 230 (Calories from Fat 80); Total Fat 9g (Saturated Fat 2g; Trans Fat 0g); Cholesterol 0mg; Sodium 210mg; Total Carbohydrate 35g (Dietary Fiber 1g; Sugars 21g); Protein 2g **% Daily Value:** Vitamin A 0%; Vitamin C 0%; Calcium 2%; Iron 8% **Exchanges:** 1/2 Starch, 2 Other Carbohydrate, 1 1/2 Fat **Carbohydrate Choices:** 2

Gingerbread Wedges

Prep Time: 15 minutes | **Start to Finish:** 45 minutes | 4 wedges

WEDGES

1 1/2 cups Original Bisquick® mix

1/4 cup packed brown sugar

2 tablespoons molasses

1 tablespoon low-fat buttermilk

1/2 teaspoon ground cinnamon

1/4 teaspoon ground ginger

1 egg or 2 egg whites

GLAZE

1/4 cup powdered sugar

1 1/2 teaspoons butter, melted (do not use margarine)

1/4 teaspoon grated lemon peel

1/2 teaspoon lemon juice

1 Heat oven to 350°F. Spray cookie sheet with cooking spray. In small bowl, mix all wedges ingredients until soft dough forms. Place on surface sprinkled with Bisquick mix; roll in Bisquick mix to coat.

2 Shape dough into ball; knead 10 times. Pat dough into 4-inch round on cookie sheet. Cut into 4 wedges; separate wedges by at least 2 inches.

3 Bake 12 to 15 minutes or until wedges are set and begin to brown. Cool 15 minutes.

4 Meanwhile, in small bowl, mix powdered sugar, butter and lemon peel. Stir in lemon juice until smooth enough to drizzle.

5 Drizzle glaze over warm wedges. Carefully separate wedges. Serve warm.

tip for *two*

The lemon, molasses and ginger team up to create a wonderful dessert. If you don't have lemon on hand, try orange juice and orange peel instead.

1 Wedge: Calories 330 (Calories from Fat 80); Total Fat 9g (Saturated Fat 3g; Trans Fat 1g); Cholesterol 55mg; Sodium 680mg; Total Carbohydrate 57g (Dietary Fiber 0g; Sugars 30g); Protein 5g   **% Daily Value:** Vitamin A 2%; Vitamin C 0%; Calcium 15%; Iron 15%   **Exchanges:** 1 1/2 Starch, 2 1/2 Other Carbohydrate, 1 1/2 Fat   **Carbohydrate Choices:** 4

Glazed Lemon-Coconut Bars

Prep Time: 15 minutes | **Start to Finish:** 1 hour 35 minutes | 8 bars

BARS

1/2 cup Bisquick Heart Smart™ mix

1 tablespoon powdered sugar

1 tablespoon firm butter or margarine

1/3 cup granulated sugar

2 tablespoons flaked coconut

1 1/2 teaspoons Bisquick Heart Smart™ mix

1 teaspoon grated lemon peel

1 tablespoon lemon juice

1 egg or 2 egg whites

LEMON GLAZE

1/4 cup powdered sugar

1 1/2 teaspoons lemon juice

1 Heat oven to 350°F. In small bowl, mix 1/2 cup Bisquick mix and 1 tablespoon powdered sugar. Cut in butter, using pastry blender (or pulling 2 table knives through ingredients in opposite directions), until crumbly. Press in ungreased 8 × 4-inch loaf pan. Bake about 10 minutes or until light brown.

2 Meanwhile, in small bowl, mix remaining bar ingredients.

3 Pour coconut mixture over baked layer. Bake about 20 minutes longer or until set and golden brown. Loosen edges from sides of pan while warm.

4 In small bowl, stir all glaze ingredients until smooth; spread over bars. Cool completely, about 1 hour. For bars, cut into 4 rows by 2 rows.

tip for *two*

You will need one small lemon to get enough peel and juice for these bars. Cut bars into mini squares, and serve with coffee or tea.

1 Bar: Calories 110 (Calories from Fat 30); Total Fat 3g (Saturated Fat 1.5g; Trans Fat 0g); Cholesterol 30mg; Sodium 105mg; Total Carbohydrate 19g (Dietary Fiber 0g; Sugars 14g); Protein 1g   **% Daily Value:** Vitamin A 0%; Vitamin C 0%; Calcium 4%; Iron 2%   **Exchanges:** 1 1/2 Other Carbohydrate, 1/2 Fat   **Carbohydrate Choices:** 1

Rich Peanut Butter Cookies

Prep Time: 30 minutes | **Start to Finish:** 30 minutes | About 1 dozen cookies

1/2 cup packed brown sugar

1/4 cup peanut butter

1/4 cup butter or margarine, softened

1 egg or 2 egg whites

2/3 cup all-purpose flour

1/4 teaspoon baking soda

1/4 teaspoon baking powder

1/8 teaspoon salt

1/2 cup peanut butter chips

1 tablespoon granulated sugar

1 Heat oven to 375°F. In medium bowl, beat brown sugar, peanut butter, butter and egg with electric mixer on medium speed until creamy, or mix with spoon. Stir in flour, baking soda, baking powder and salt. Stir in peanut butter chips.

2 Shape dough into 1 1/2-inch balls. Dip tops of balls into granulated sugar. On ungreased cookie sheet, place balls, sugared sides up, about 3 inches apart (do not flatten).

3 Bake 9 to 10 minutes or until light brown. Cool 5 minutes; remove from cookie sheet to cooling rack.

tip for *two*

This is the perfect cookie recipe for two because it makes only one dozen cookies. If you prefer more, you can easily double the recipe. Why not try semisweet or milk chocolate chips instead of the peanut butter chips?

1 Cookie: Calories 180 (Calories from Fat 80); Total Fat 9g (Saturated Fat 3.5g; Trans Fat 0g); Cholesterol 30mg; Sodium 140mg; Total Carbohydrate 20g (Dietary Fiber 0g; Sugars 13g); Protein 4g **% Daily Value:** Vitamin A 2%; Vitamin C 0%; Calcium 2%; Iron 4% **Exchanges:** 1 Starch, 1/2 Other Carbohydrate, 1 1/2 Fat **Carbohydrate Choices:** 1

Chocolate–Chocolate Chip Cookies

Prep Time: 30 minutes | **Start to Finish:** 30 minutes | 2 dozen (2-inch) cookies

1/2 cup packed brown sugar

3 tablespoons butter or margarine, softened

1/2 teaspoon vanilla

1 egg

1/2 cup all-purpose flour

3 tablespoons unsweetened baking cocoa

1/2 teaspoon baking soda

Dash salt

1/2 cup semisweet chocolate chips

1 Heat oven to 375°F. In large bowl, beat brown sugar and butter with electric mixer on medium speed until light and fluffy, or mix with spoon. Beat in vanilla and egg.

2 Stir in flour, cocoa, baking soda and salt. Stir in chocolate chips. Onto ungreased cookie sheet, drop dough by teaspoonfuls about 2 inches apart.

3 Bake 8 to 9 minutes or until set (do not overbake). Cool 1 minute; remove from cookie sheet to cooling rack.

tip for *two*

Turn these cookies into bars. Heat oven to 375°F. Lightly grease bottom and sides of 8-inch square pan with cooking spray. Make dough as directed; press in pan. Bake 12 to 15 minutes or until set (do not overbake). Cool completely. For bars, cut into 6 rows by 4 rows.

1 Cookie: Calories 70 (Calories from Fat 25); Total Fat 3g (Saturated Fat 1.5g; Trans Fat 0g); Cholesterol 15mg; Sodium 50mg; Total Carbohydrate 9g (Dietary Fiber 0g; Sugars 6g); Protein 0g   **% Daily Value:** Vitamin A 0%; Vitamin C 0%; Calcium 0%; Iron 2%   **Exchanges:** 1/2 Starch, 1/2 Fat   **Carbohydrate Choices:** 1/2

1 Honey-Coffee Ice Cream Topper

Drizzle honey over vanilla ice cream or frozen yogurt; sprinkle with plain or flavored instant coffee granules.

2 Maple-Citrus Fruit

Mix a bit of maple syrup or honey with grated lemon, lime or orange peel and juice; drizzle over sliced bananas or other fresh fruit.

3 White or Dark Chocolate Drizzle

Heat white vanilla baking chips or semisweet chocolate chips until melted; drizzle over strawberries, frozen yogurt or chocolate cookies.

4 Raspberry Cream Tart

Fill graham cracker tart shells with vanilla pudding; top with whipped cream and fresh raspberries.

5 Easy Parfait

Layer any flavor of yogurt or pudding, ready-to-eat cereal, coarsely chopped cookies or cake pieces, berries or sliced fresh fruit and whipped topping in a tall glass to make an easy parfait.

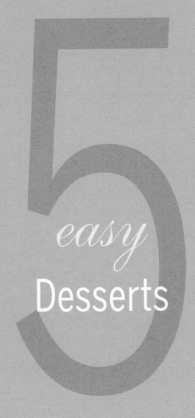

5 easy Desserts

Everyone loves a sweet treat once in a while. You can make simple desserts sensational with these quick and easy ideas.

Choose Good Food for Good Health

Food is one of life's greatest pleasures. Eating healthy means choosing and enjoying a balance and variety of foods and keeping your body healthy with the foods you eat. Can enjoying food and eating healthy go together? Yes! And it may be even easier to start eating healthy now that you're cooking for two.

The Nutrients in Foods

The foods we eat are made up of these major nutrients, each with its own special and important function:

- **Protein** builds and repairs muscles, skin and other structural parts of the body. Every organ in the body is made from protein. You can get protein from lean meats, poultry, fish; legumes; and fat-free and low-fat dairy products.
- **Carbohydrate** supplies energy for activity. Even when you're sleeping, carbohydrate fuels ongoing body functions. Fiber, found in many carbohydrate foods, helps maintain a healthy digestive tract and heart. You can get carbohydrate from bran cereals and whole-grain breads, beans, legumes, vegetables and fruits.
- **Fat** supplies what the body needs to make hormones, keep skin healthy and support the nervous system. Different types of fats have different health benefits. You can get fat from olive oil, canola oil, other vegetable oils and nuts.
- **Vitamins** help release energy from the protein, fat and carbohydrate you eat. Your vision, hair, skin and bone strength all depend on the vitamins you eat. The more variety of foods you eat, the more likely you are to get all the vitamins your body needs.
- **Minerals** help your body carry oxygen to the cells (iron) and build strong bones and teeth (calcium). The best way to get enough minerals is by eating a variety of foods.

Adopt a Healthy Lifestyle

A healthy lifestyle can help you look and feel better. Another important consideration is that healthy eating can promote independence by helping protect you from illness. Eating well and being good to your body can reduce the risk of heart disease, diabetes, certain cancers and obesity. What does having a healthy lifestyle mean?

It may take just a few small steps to improve your lifestyle habits. When making changes, take one step or one change at a time. When the first step is mastered, take another step. These little changes add up and make a big difference when trying to eat healthier and the benefits that go along with that, like having more energy and feeling good about yourself.

Eat Breakfast

It sets the stage for the rest of the day in terms of energy and nutrition. People who eat breakfast tend to have healthier diets, ones that contain more vitamins, minerals and fiber and less fat. Breakfast eaters are also more apt to have better control over their weight.

Eat Smaller Meals Each Day

Eating every three or four hours may help keep energy up and hunger pangs at bay. Eating less than that can make it very difficult for you to get all the nutrition you need. In each meal, include a little protein from lean meats, nuts and low-fat dairy foods. And, eat only when you're hungry.

Work in Snacks

Though myths persist that snacking might get in the way of healthy eating, those between-meal snacks can be just what you need to boost your energy and your health. Eating small wholesome snacks is a smart way to spread calories over the course of the day. Choose whole grains for energy, lean protein to help extend that energy and fiber-rich foods to fill you up but not out. Easy good-for-you snacks can be a quick pick-me-up and keep between-meal hunger to a minimum. (See 5 Easy On-the-Go Snacks, page 23.)

Increase Your Fiber

Nutrition experts recommend eating at least 25 grams of fiber every day. For long-lasting energy, to feel more satisfied and to have a healthy digestive system, choose fiber-rich foods such as whole-grain cereals, legumes, beans, whole grains, fruits and vegetables.

Choose Brightly Colored Fruits and Vegetables

Fruits and vegetables deliver color, and the most colorful often contain the most nutrients. Each fruit and vegetable contains a unique set of vitamins, minerals and phytonutrients (naturally occurring substances with health-helping benefits). Aim for five to nine choices a day; if that's too hard to achieve all at once, start by increasing the amount you eat now.

Picture Your Portions

What do sensible portions look like? Most are probably smaller than you'd think! To start, measure your portions; soon you'll be able to "eyeball" them accurately. Use familiar objects to help you visualize, like:

3-ounce serving of meat or poultry	= Size of a deck of cards or a cassette tape
1-ounce cube of cheese	= Size of your thumb or 2 dominoes
1 ounce of nuts	= Fits into the cupped palm of a child's hand
1 cup	= Size of a woman's fist; cereal that fills half of a standard cereal bowl
1/2 cup	= A fruit or vegetable that fits into the palm of your hand, about the size of a tennis ball
1 tablespoon	= Size of your thumb tip (tip to middle joint)
1 teaspoon	= Size of your fingertip (tip to middle joint)

Teach yourself how much your favorite utensils hold, so that you know how much "one ladleful" of soup, for example, actually contains. Just fill the utensil with water, then pour the water out into a measuring cup.

Get used to what a portion looks like in a particular bowl or plate—say, a 1/2-cup serving of cereal in a bowl—then use that same bowl every time you serve that cereal.

Fill two-thirds of your plate with plant-based foods like grains, fruits, vegetables, nuts or beans. The remaining third can contain meat, poultry, fish, eggs and dairy.

Serve meals on smaller plates. Most of us eat what is on our plate, so starting with a smaller plate may help you control the amount of food you eat.

Be Active

Being active just feels good, doesn't it? Bored, or need a new routine? Take a brisk walk, go for a swim, dance to a favorite song—try to be active in some way every day. Exercising regularly helps: build healthy muscles, joints and bones; you relax and clear your mind; you sleep better; keep you in good spirits. Being active 30 to 60 minutes each day is recommended, and it's okay to break up the time into smaller time segments—that's still beneficial for your heart and other muscles.

Increase your activity by doing housework, walking to the store and parking farther away when running errands. When sitting and knitting, reading or working at a computer, it's a good idea to get up and walk around for a bit every hour or so to clear your mind and get your muscles moving.

Eat More Fish

Experts recommend eating fish once or twice a week. Salmon and other fatty fish, like tuna and herring, have been getting a lot of attention lately because of the omega-3 fatty acids they contain, a fat that is beneficial for heart health. Most fish are also low in calories, very low in saturated fat and high in polyunsaturated fat. These fats are good because they tend not to raise cholesterol levels like saturated fat does.

Drink Water

Water aids nearly every function of your body. Water and other calorie-free fluids help cool your body, keep it functioning normally and aid in getting rid of waste. Drink six to eight glasses of water every day to stay hydrated. Beverages can boost your nutrition if you choose a healthy drink, like fat-free or low-fat milk or soymilk, tea (herbal, green or black) and 100-percent fruit juice. Save non-nutritious beverages (such as soda) for between meals. Drink fluids often during the day. The next time you feel tired and cranky between meals, try drinking water or another beverage instead of eating. You may just be thirsty.

Choose Meatless Meals

To help reduce the amount of saturated fat and calories in your diet, eating a meatless meal at least once a week may appeal to you. Instead of meat, try kidney or garbanzo beans, legumes, tofu, pasta and whole grains. To get started, see the list of meatless recipes at the end of this section.

Getting Started

Many of us want to eat healthier, whether just to feel better or to drop a few pounds. But with our fast-paced lives, getting started can be a challenge. This cookbook makes it easy by providing good-for-you recipes.

The Recipes

The recipes in this cookbook were selected for two-person families. Many contain fruits, vegetables, beans and whole grains, and most fall within recommended lower levels for fat and sodium.

Canola and olive oils are called for throughout the book. They were chosen because they are health-wise fats to use for stir-frying, cooking and some baking. Because butter yields a tender product and gives great flavor to baked goods, you'll see butter used in the desserts chapter (although at a lower level than in many cookbooks).

Fat-free, or skim, milk is used as an easy way to cut fat. Depending on the fat and calorie content of each dish, reduced-fat and fat-free dairy ingredients, like cream cheese and sour cream, may be called for. If a particular recipe is reasonable in fat content and calories, the regular product is used. If you usually use reduced-fat or fat-free products, you may try them instead. To reduce sodium, use lower-sodium soups and other products.

Eggs are used because they contain many nutrients, protein, iron, vitamins and minerals; you can use egg whites or egg substitutes instead of whole eggs.

In Your Kitchen

You can make a big difference in reducing fat, sodium, cholesterol and calories when you select and cook fresh, healthy foods. Here's how:

- Cut down on the total amount of fat and saturated fat. Think liquid and use canola or olive oil rather than solid butter, shortening or margarine.
- Cook without fat—braise, steam, poach or bake. Grilling, broiling and using a table-top grill are also good methods because they allow fat to drip off.
- Read food labels to compare sodium levels. Pick no-salt-added or low-sodium broths and other foods when you'd like to cut back. Don't add salt at the table, and don't cook potatoes, pasta or rice in salted water.
- Season the foods you prepare with herbs, lemon juice, vinegar, chopped fresh or dried herbs, chopped fresh chiles, sautéed chopped onions, garlic, gingerroot, spices and juices instead of salt.

- Boost the amount of potassium you eat to balance out the sodium. Eat foods that deliver potassium, including bananas, peaches, tuna, beans, spinach and tomatoes.
- If you'd like to reduce cholesterol, you can use egg whites and egg substitutes instead of whole eggs. Also increase cholesterol-lowering foods, like oats, barley and other grains.
- Eat more vegetables and fruits. Add vegetables to stir-fries, soups and salads. Eat fruit as a snack or dessert, either alone, paired with cheese or prepared in a recipe.
- Add grains, legumes and beans to soups, stews and stir-fries to increase fiber and add texture.

So you can make the best choice possible, each recipe also lists per serving the calories, calories from fat, fat, saturated fat, cholesterol, sodium, carbohydrate, dietary fiber and protein and % Daily Value for calcium, iron and vitamins A and C. Because of the ingredients used, many of the recipes in this cookbook:

- Contain less sodium (main-dish recipes that contain less than 715 milligrams of sodium per serving)
- Are high in fiber (contain 3 or more grams of fiber per serving)
- Are high in calcium (contain more than 10% Daily Value of calcium per serving)
- Contain less cholesterol (contain less than 75 milligrams of cholesterol per serving)
- Are high in iron (contain more than 10% Daily Value of iron per serving)

Meatless Recipes

Helpful Nutrition and Cooking Information

Nutrition Guidelines

We provide nutrition information for each recipe, including calories, fat, cholesterol, sodium, carbohydrate, fiber and protein.

Recommended intake for a daily diet of 2,000 calories as set by the Food and Drug Administration

Total Fat	Less than 65g
Saturated Fat	Less than 20g
Cholesterol	Less than 300mg
Sodium	Less than 2,400mg
Total Carbohydrate	300g
Dietary Fiber	25g

Criteria Used for Calculating Nutrition Information

- The first ingredient was used wherever a choice is given (such as 1/3 cup sour cream or plain yogurt).
- The first ingredient amount was used wherever a range is given (such as 3- to 3 1/2-pound cut-up broiler-fryer chicken).
- The first serving number was used wherever a range is given (such as 4 to 6 servings).
- "If desired" ingredients and recipe variations were not included (such as sprinkle with brown sugar, if desired).
- Only the amount of a marinade or frying oil that is estimated to be absorbed by the food during preparation or cooking was calculated.

Ingredients Used in Recipe Testing and Nutrition Calculations

- Ingredients used for testing represent those that the majority of consumers use: large eggs, 2% milk, 80%-lean ground beef, canned ready-to-use chicken broth and vegetable oil spread containing not less than 65 percent fat.
- Fat-free, low-fat or low-sodium products were not used, unless indicated.
- Solid vegetable shortening (not butter, margarine, nonstick cooking sprays or vegetable oil spread as they can cause sticking problems) was used to grease pans, unless indicated.

Equipment Used in Recipe Testing

We use equipment for testing that the majority of consumers use. If a specific piece of equipment (such as a wire whisk) is necessary for recipe success, it is listed in the recipe.

- Cookware and bakeware without nonstick coatings were used, unless indicated.
- No dark-colored, black or insulated bakeware was used.
- When a pan is specified in a recipe, a metal pan was used; a baking dish or pie plate means ovenproof glass was used.
- An electric hand mixer was used for mixing when mixer speeds are specified in the recipe. When a mixer speed is not given, a spoon or fork was used.

Cooking Terms Glossary

Beat: Mix ingredients vigorously with spoon, fork, wire whisk, hand beater or electric mixer until smooth and uniform.

Boil: Heat liquid until bubbles rise continuously and break on the surface and steam is given off. For rolling boil, the bubbles form rapidly.

Chop: Cut into coarse or fine irregular pieces with a knife, food chopper, blender or food processor.

Cube: Cut into squares 1/2 inch or larger.

Dice: Cut into squares smaller than 1/2 inch.

Grate: Cut into tiny particles using small rough holes of grater (citrus peel or chocolate).

Grease: Rub the inside surface of a pan with shortening, using pastry brush, piece of waxed paper or paper towel, to prevent food from sticking during baking (as for some casseroles).

Julienne: Cut into thin, matchlike strips, using knife or food processor (vegetables, fruits, meats).

Mix: Combine ingredients in any way that distributes them evenly.

Sauté: Cook foods in hot oil or margarine over medium-high heat with frequent tossing and turning motion.

Shred: Cut into long thin pieces by rubbing food across the holes of a shredder, as for cheese, or by using a knife to slice very thinly, as for cabbage.

Simmer: Cook in liquid just below the boiling point on top of the stove; usually after reducing heat from a boil. Bubbles will rise slowly and break just below the surface.

Stir: Mix ingredients until uniform consistency. Stir once in a while for stirring occasionally, often for stirring frequently and continuously for stirring constantly.

Toss: Tumble ingredients (such as green salad) lightly with a lifting motion, usually to coat evenly or mix with another food.

Metric Conversion Guide

Volume

U.S. Units	Canadian Metric	Australian Metric
1/4 teaspoon	1 mL	1 ml
1/2 teaspoon	2 mL	2 ml
1 teaspoon	5 mL	5 ml
1 tablespoon	15 mL	20 ml
1/4 cup	50 mL	60 ml
1/3 cup	75 mL	80 ml
1/2 cup	125 mL	125 ml
2/3 cup	150 mL	170 ml
3/4 cup	175 mL	190 ml
1 cup	250 mL	250 ml
1 quart	1 liter	1 liter
1 1/2 quarts	1.5 liters	1.5 liters
2 quarts	2 liters	2 liters
2 1/2 quarts	2.5 liters	2.5 liters
3 quarts	3 liters	3 liters
4 quarts	4 liters	4 liters

Weight

U.S. Units	Canadian Metric	Australian Metric
1 ounce	30 grams	30 grams
2 ounces	55 grams	60 grams
3 ounces	85 grams	90 grams
4 ounces (1/4 pound)	115 grams	125 grams
8 ounces (1/2 pound)	225 grams	225 grams
16 ounces (1 pound)	455 grams	500 grams
1 pound	455 grams	1/2 kilogram

Measurements

Inches	Centimeters
1	2.5
2	5.0
3	7.5
4	10.0
5	12.5
6	15.0
7	17.5
8	20.5
9	23.0
10	25.5
11	28.0
12	30.5
13	33.0

Temperatures

Fahrenheit	Celsius
32°	0°
212°	100°
250°	120°
275°	140°
300°	150°
325°	160°
350°	180°
375°	190°
400°	200°
425°	220°
450°	230°
475°	240°
500°	260°

Note: The recipes in this cookbook have not been developed or tested using metric measures. When converting recipes to metric, some variations in quality may be noted.

Index

Complete your cookbook library with these *Betty Crocker* titles

Betty Crocker Baking for Today

Betty Crocker Basics

Betty Crocker's Best Bread Machine Cookbook

Betty Crocker's Best Chicken Cookbook

Betty Crocker's Best Christmas Cookbook

Betty Crocker's Best of Baking

Betty Crocker's Best of Healthy and Hearty Cooking

Betty Crocker's Best-Loved Recipes

Betty Crocker's Bisquick® Cookbook

Betty Crocker Bisquick® II Cookbook

Betty Crocker Bisquick® Impossibly Easy Pies

Betty Crocker Celebrate!

Betty Crocker's Complete Thanksgiving Cookbook

Betty Crocker's Cook Book for Boys and Girls

Betty Crocker's Cook It Quick

Betty Crocker Cookbook, 10th Edition— *The* **BIG RED** *Cookbook*®

Betty Crocker Cookbook, Bridal Edition

Betty Crocker's Cookie Book

Betty Crocker's Cooking Basics

Betty Crocker's Cooking for Two

Betty Crocker's Cooky Book, Facsimile Edition

Betty Crocker Decorating Cakes and Cupcakes

Betty Crocker's Diabetes Cookbook

Betty Crocker Dinner Made Easy with Rotisserie Chicken

Betty Crocker Easy Everyday Vegetarian

Betty Crocker Easy Family Dinners

Betty Crocker's Easy Slow Cooker Dinners

Betty Crocker's Eat and Lose Weight

Betty Crocker's Entertaining Basics

Betty Crocker's Flavors of Home

Betty Crocker 4-Ingredient Dinners

Betty Crocker Grilling Made Easy

Betty Crocker Healthy Heart Cookbook

Betty Crocker's Healthy New Choices

Betty Crocker's Indian Home Cooking

Betty Crocker's Italian Cooking

Betty Crocker's Kids Cook!

Betty Crocker's Kitchen Library

Betty Crocker's Living with Cancer Cookbook

Betty Crocker Low-Carb Lifestyle Cookbook

Betty Crocker's Low-Fat, Low-Cholesterol Cooking Today

Betty Crocker More Slow Cooker Recipes

Betty Crocker's New Cake Decorating

Betty Crocker's New Chinese Cookbook

Betty Crocker One-Dish Meals

Betty Crocker's A Passion for Pasta

Betty Crocker's Picture Cook Book, Facsimile Edition

Betty Crocker's Quick & Easy Cookbook

Betty Crocker's Slow Cooker Cookbook

Betty Crocker's Ultimate Cake Mix Cookbook

Betty Crocker's Vegetarian Cooking

Betty Crocker Why It Works

Betty Crocker Win at Weight Loss Cookbook

Cocina Betty Crocker